D1460131

 libraries

Pollokshaws Library
50/60 Shawbridge Street
Glasgow G43 1RW
Phone: 0141 276 1535 Fax 276 1536

This book is due for return on or before the last date shown below. It may
be renewed by telephone, personal application, fax or post, quoting this
date, author, title and the book number

13 MAY 2023 WITHDRAWN

Glasgow Life and its service brands, including Glasgow
Libraries, (found at www.glasgowlife.org.uk) are operating
names for Culture and Sport Glasgow

Disaster before D-Day

Disaster before D-Day

Unravelling the Tragedy at Slapton Sands

by
Stephen Wynn

Pen & Sword
MILITARY

AN IMPRINT OF PEN & SWORD BOOKS LTD.
YORKSHIRE – PHILADELPHIA

First published in Great Britain in 2019 by
Pen & Sword Military
An imprint of
Pen & Sword Books Ltd
Yorkshire - Philadelphia

Copyright © Stephen Wynn, 2019

ISBN 978 1 52673 511 9

The right of Stephen Wynn to be identified as Author of this work has been
asserted by him in accordance with the Copyright, Designs and Patents Act 1988.

A CIP catalogue record for this book is
available from the British Library.

All rights reserved. No part of this book may be reproduced or transmitted in any
form or by any means, electronic or mechanical including photocopying, recording
or by any information storage and retrieval system, without permission from the
Publisher in writing.

Printed and bound in England
By TJ International Ltd.

Pen & Sword Books Ltd incorporates the Imprints of Pen & Sword Books
Archaeology, Atlas, Aviation, Battleground, Discovery, Family History, History,
Maritime, Military, Naval, Politics, Railways, Select, Transport, True Crime,
Fiction, Frontline Books, Leo Cooper, Praetorian Press, Seaforth Publishing,
Wharncliffe and White Owl.

For a complete list of Pen & Sword titles please contact

PEN & SWORD BOOKS LIMITED
47 Church Street, Barnsley, South Yorkshire, S70 2AS, England
E-mail: enquiries@pen-and-sword.co.uk
Website: www.pen-and-sword.co.uk

or

PEN AND SWORD BOOKS
1950 Lawrence Rd, Havertown, PA 19083, USA
E-mail: uspen-and-sword@casematepublishers.com
Website: www.penandswordbooks.com

Contents

Biography

Stephen is a happily retired police officer having served with Essex Police as a constable for thirty years, between 1983 and 2013. He is married to Tanya who is also his best friend.

Both his sons, Luke and Ross, were members of the armed forces, collectively serving five tours of Afghanistan between 2008 and 2013. Both were injured on their first tour. This led to Stephen's first book, *Two Sons in a Warzone – Afghanistan: The True Story of a Fathers Conflict*, which was published in October 2010.

Both of his grandfathers served in and survived the First World War, one with the Royal Irish Rifles, the other in the Mercantile Navy, while his father was a member of the Royal Army Ordinance Corp during the Second World War.

Stephen collaborated with one of his writing partners, Ken Porter, on a previous book published in August 2012, *German PoW Camp 266 – Langdon Hills*, which spent six weeks as the number one best-selling book in Waterstones, Basildon between March and April 2013. Steve and Ken collaborated on a further four books in the Towns & Cities in the Great War series by Pen & Sword. Stephen has also written other titles in the same series of books, and in February 2017, *The Surrender of Singapore – Three Years of Hell 1942-45*, was published and *Against All Odds – Walter Tull – The Black Lieutenant*, followed in March 2018.

Stephen has also co-written three crime thrillers which were published between 2010 and 2012, and center round a fictional detective, named Terry Danvers.

When he is not writing, Tanya and he enjoy the simplicity of walking their four German Shepherd dogs early each morning when most sensible people are still fast asleep in their beds.

Chapter One

The 1938 military exercise at Slapton Sands

W hen Slapton Sands is mentioned in a historical sense, most people almost immediately connect it to the tragedy that occurred there and in the waters of Lyme Bay on 27 and 28 April 1944, when a large number of American soldiers and sailors lost their lives.

But there had been a previous military exercise at Slapton Sands in July 1938. This was mainly due to the insistence of Brigadier Bernard Montgomery who, despite British politicians trying to play down the relationship between Britain and Germany, foresaw the potential troubles ahead. Even earlier than that, in 1936, there had been an exercise at Swanage, as Nazi Germany began to flex its military muscles. Nobody wanted a war, except maybe Germany, but it had become a case of train for the worst while hoping for the best.

On Tuesday, 5 July 1938, as darkness fell across Slapton Sands, everything appeared to be normal on this stretch of the quiet Devon coastline, but in the early hours of Wednesday, its usual peace and tranquillity were suddenly broken as it became the scene of one of the biggest military exercises in the history of the nation, and certainly the biggest that had ever taken place in the West Country. It was a combined exercise which included the British Army, Navy and Air Force.

As the exercise got underway, military observers were watching keenly from inland vantage points.

There was a big difference between the exercises of 1938 and 1944 at Slapton Sands. The 1944 version was a practice for the invasion of German-occupied Europe on the beaches of Normandy, while the 1938 version was of a defensive nature, designed to deal with the threat of a German invasion of the UK mainland.

For the purposes of the exercise, the invading forces had selected Slapton Sands due to its long shingle beach where men and vehicles could be safely landed.

In the early hours of 6 July 1938, it looked like the planned exercise wasn't going to go ahead due to the inclement weather, but as the day progressed the weather improved, the wind dropped, and although there was a considerable swell further out in the English Channel, the waters of Start Bay were reasonably calm.

The exercise, which had first been spoken about a year earlier, had as its main objective the investigation of the tactical and technical aspects of an enemy amphibious landing, paying special attention to the potential seaward approach and attacking options having landed on the beach.

The pretend story and background to the exercise was thus: Wessex (Blueland), which is made up from the counties of Cornwall, Devon, Dorset, and Somerset, was being invaded by Eastland (Redland), which comprised what are often referred to collectively as the Home Counties: Berkshire, Buckinghamshire, Essex, Hertfordshire, Kent, Surrey, and Sussex. Also on their side was East Anglia, which included the counties of Norfolk, Suffolk, and parts of Cambridgeshire and Essex.

The presumption was that Eastland was much the stronger force and the chances of a successful landing and the subsequent occupation of a considerable area of land were more than just a probability.

The defenders of Wessex in the main consisted of the 2nd Battalion, Gloucestershire Regiment. Their platoons and sections were situated at a number of points a few miles inland at Higher Coltscombe, the road junction at Whitestone Cross, and the high ground which was just east of East Down. They only had machine guns and rifles at their disposal, with no artillery or tanks. This would be somewhat unrealistic and why such pieces of important equipment were missing wasn't explained. Maybe it was because they didn't want to damage any of the roads in the area that were most definitely not designed to cater for such heavy vehicles. Elements of the Territorial Army also took part in the exercise by occupying the Plymouth Fortress.

The landings took place across three beaches of the Wessex coastline. The invading forces were made up of one company of the East Yorkshire Regiment, which hit the shore in the vicinity of Matthews Point, with their eventual inland target being Dartmouth; two companies of the Lincolnshire Regiment landed at Strete Gate; and two companies of the King's Own Scottish Borderers came ashore on the beaches at Slapton Sands, immediately opposite the hotel. All attacking soldiers landed with their bayonets fixed. On the beaches at Strete Gate, engineers with the attacking units constructed two piers and a roadway to accommodate the landing of personnel, heavy equipment and supporting vehicles.

Although the exercise was set up predominantly to develop a defensive strategy in the case of an actual wartime amphibious landing of an enemy force, there were also lessons to be learnt from the 'enemy's' perspective.

An example of this was that a certain number of the invading force were nominated as casualties. They were initially treated where they fell on the beach, and then were conveyed back to a waiting ship that was sitting in Lyme Bay. This was flawed for various reasons. Firstly, in any real invasion, there would, in all probability, already be in place robust defensive structures that would include machine-gun positions, artillery units, aircraft and tanks, and more than likely naval vessels would be making their way to the location at top speed. There would be hundreds if not thousands of wounded attacking soldiers strewn across the beach. Trying to effectively and safely deal with so many casualties in such a short period of time, while explosions and gunfire were going off all around, would have been very dangerous and life threatening. Many medics would have been required and trained medics were a much-needed commodity. As for then attempting to carry wounded personnel to a nearby boat on the shoreline to transfer them to a waiting ship, while machine-gun fire was flying all around, artillery shells exploding and aircraft attacking, just wasn't practical. How many men did you put on the waiting craft before it left, and who decided? Deploying such a tactic would end up causing more problems than it was solving.

Sadly, in such circumstances all that could be done was to treat wounded men where they fell as best that they could: get them to some kind of cover if possible before moving on to the next man, just hoping that they would still be alive once the attack was over. As with medics, so with ordinary soldiers: If one or two men stopped to help a wounded colleague, they immediately placed themselves in danger by making themselves static targets. Moreover if say one hundred men become casualties and two men stop to help each of them, in a short time that is three hundred men who are then not involved in the attack, which could result in failure.

Medics were some of the bravest men on D-Day. I spoke briefly with an elderly gentleman in June 2017 who was then 94. On 6 June 1944 he was a 21-year-old medic in the Royal Marines, and one of the thousands of men who were landed on Gold and Sword beaches.

Many of his memories of that day have partly faded with the passage of time, whilst others, he tries to forget and bury deep within himself; like a photograph album that we know is there, but choose not to open anymore. He tries his best to forget the dreadful sights he saw that day; the faces of friends and colleagues who died in his arms as he tried to save them. A very brave, modest and unassuming gentleman if ever there was one. A man whom most of his neighbours know little about, and certainly nothing of the numerous acts of unselfish bravery he carried out on the beaches of Normandy all those years ago, which is just the way he would like it to remain.

To make the landing part of the exercise a success, the number of men deployed in defending the attack was scaled down somewhat.

There was much air activity on both sides, with the defending forces of Wessex sending out numerous aircraft to undertake reconnaissance flights and locate the enemy fleet. Among them would be a number of bomber aircraft whose job it was to locate and destroy Eastland's aircraft carrier, HMS *Courageous*, from which the attacking forces ran the aerial side of their operation. This involved the use of Swordfish bomber aircraft – biplanes almost from another era – provided by number 12 Squadron, Fleet Air Arm.

There were lighter moments during the operation, which I feel are worth a mention:

During the exercise's preliminary arrangements at Portsmouth, a group of Indian Lascars, or workers, who had been engaging the ships at the docks, threatened to go on strike because they did not want to put on gas masks, and for some reason believed that they were being sent out to Spain, of all places.

There was a somewhat unusual if not slightly humorous ending to the exercise when, owing to bad weather, it had to be cancelled. This resulted in more than 1,000 soldiers, officers and naval ratings – most of the Eastland forces – having to be rushed to the Royal Naval College Dartmouth in the early hours of Thursday, 7 July, after the re-embarkation at Slapton Sands had been cancelled. Companies of the Middlesex Regiment had been safely conveyed to HMS *Lancashire* before the order to abandon the operation was given. Earlier in the day, after the invading forces had been given the order to retreat, it was decided that if the sea was too rough, then re-embarkation would take place from the much calmer waters of Dartmouth Harbour the following day, but it would not count as part of the exercise. Late on the Wednesday evening it became obvious to everybody that re-embarkation of 2,500 troops retreating from the beaches of Slapton Sands would be risky because of a severe decline in the weather. There were real concerns that if the re-embarkation continued, soldiers could end up being injured or killed, which was felt not to be a risk worth taking on a non-wartime training exercise. It was decided that the best course of action was to find shelter for them on land. Instead, the soldiers who had not been picked up by HMS *Lancashire* before the order to abandon the exercise was given then had to march the five miles into Dartmouth in the pouring rain where they were accommodated at the Royal Naval College. This, after a tiring day, was much appreciated. By the time they had all arrived, every spare bit of floor space was taken. After a reasonable night's sleep, or as good as it could get sleeping on a cold hard floor, the ratings embarked from Dartmouth on a destroyer, while the soldiers left in a combination of trucks and specially organised trains that conveyed them to Weymouth.

The winners of the exercise were ultimately deemed to be the defending troops of Wessex, who would have, if it had been an actual invasion, undoubtedly won the day. If the retreating troops of Eastland had actually been unable to re-embark from the beaches at Slapton Sands, those stranded there would have either been killed or taken prisoner.

How much was learned from the exercise is unclear, but Slapton Sands were certainly remembered when the time came for the Americans to begin their training for D-Day and a location similar to Utah Beach in Normandy was needed. It was in fact Montgomery who had recognised the similarities between the two beaches and suggested Slapton.

Chapter Two

Planning for Operation Overlord

To keep both sides happy, the deputy to General Eisenhower would have to be a British officer, with the title of Chief of Staff to the Supreme Allied Commander, or COSSAC, a position he commenced on 12 March 1943, even though the Supreme Allied Commander hadn't even been selected at that time.

The man who would fulfil this role was Lieutenant General Frederick Edgworth Morgan, who had a military career stretching back to 1913. At the outbreak of the Second World War he was promoted to brigadier and given command of the 1st Support Group of the 1st Armoured Division, which he was in charge of throughout the Battle of France during May 1940. He was further promoted to lieutenant general in May 1942.

Having passed out of the Royal Military Academy at Woolwich, Morgan was commissioned as a second lieutenant in the Royal Artillery. He served in the Battle of Ypres as well as the bloody Battle of the Somme, twice being mentioned in dispatches. As well as having to come up with a suitable plan for the invasion of German-occupied Europe, he was also tasked with coming up with an 'elaborate camouflage and deception scheme', the aim of which was to convince the Nazi leaders that the Allied invasion was going to take place before the end of 1943 and in locations other than where it subsequently took place.

One of the main decisions was where the invasion should take place. Morgan and his staff looked through reels and reels of photographs the RAF had taken of the European coastline between Vlissingen in Holland and Cherbourg in south-west France. Also taken in to account were reports from the French Resistance, tidal times, and millions of postcards of the coast of Europe that were sent in to the War Office in response to a request by the BBC.

Two locations immediately came to mind. The most obvious was the shortest distance across the Channel, the Pas-de-Calais. But this was also obvious to the Germans, so the beaches of Normandy became the chosen location for Operation Overlord.

Morgan submitted his plans for Overlord to the British and US chiefs of staff in July 1943, which they considered at the First Quebec Conference that took place between 17 and 24 August 1943 at the Citadelle, a military installation, and the Chateau Frontenac, one of Canada's grand railway hotels, in Quebec City.

Although hosted by the Canadian Prime Minister, William Lyon Mackenzie King, he played little part in the discussion. That was left to Churchill and Roosevelt. Stalin had also been invited, but was unable to for 'military reasons'.

The outcome of the conference was an agreement to plan for the invasion on 1 May 1944, meaning they had given themselves just seven and a half months to make and agree the plan, assemble and train the men, and amass all the necessary vehicles and equipment. Success would mean eventual freedom for large parts of the world; failure would mean a Nazi Germany possibly ruling the world for a very long time to come.

The Normandy Landings had also been discussed at the Third Washington Conference that was held between Roosevelt and Churchill on 12–25 May 1943. An invasion of Normandy hadn't been the only idea that had been discussed: Operation Jupiter was a plan to invade Norway and Finland vigorously pushed by Winston Churchill. Much to his surprise, one would imagine, it was wholeheartedly rejected by all of the senior British and Allied commanders. Despite its objectives of protecting Arctic convoys and freeing Norway from German occupation, it was thought to have limited value and there were concerns about the ability of the Allies to provide effective air support. Churchill didn't give up on the idea easily, but it was rejected by Roosevelt, Mountbatten, General Andrew McNaughton, commander of the 1st Canadian Infantry Division, McKenzie King and Lieutenant General Sir Frederick Morgan, chief of staff to the supreme allied commander. Churchill never gave a totally plausible reason for his continued pushing of Operation Jupiter, although there were some who believed it was to appease Stalin by opening up a second front close to the Soviet Union.

Another agreement that came out of the conference was to place more focus on pushing Italy out of the war. Operation Husky had already seen the capture of Sicily, which provided the Allies with a good foothold to attack Italy and opened up a large area of the Mediterranean Sea to Allied shipping. An unexpected effect of the Allied victory in Sicily was the need for Germany to divert a large number of her troops from the newly begun offensive at Kursk in Russia. The intended Allied invasion of mainland Italy was scheduled to begin on 3 September 1943, but the very same day an Armistice between the Allies and the Italians was signed and Italy's war was over.

The reason American troops were where they were at the time of Operation Tiger and Operation Fabius was because of the intended Allied invasion of German-occupied Europe as part of Operation Overlord.

Originally the cross-Channel attack, which it has to be said, was not everybody's first choice option, especially the British top brass, was known by the name of Operation Roundup, but as history records, this was subsequently changed to Operation Overlord.

It was at the Casablanca Conference in January 1943 that Roosevelt, on the advice of his army chief of staff General George C. Marshall, put forward a joint Allied attack across the English Channel. Winston Churchill on the other hand, on the advice of the chief of the imperial general staff, who was also the head of the British army, General Sir Alan Brooke, favoured an initial attack on Sicily followed by a full-blown invasion of mainland Italy. They weren't against an invasion of German-occupied Europe, but Churchill didn't feel at the time that the country was ready to embark on such an ordeal.

By invading Sicily and then Italy, they would be up against an inferior army rather than the might and fighting experience of the Wehrmacht. Churchill also liked the plan as it provided the opportunity of drawing German reserves away from the north of France so that when the invasion of Europe eventually took place the German army wouldn't be at its strongest, especially as at the time they were still fighting on the Eastern Front as well.

Roosevelt knew he had to tread carefully if he didn't want to alienate himself in the eyes of the American people, most of whom had never wanted to become involved in what they saw as a European war; after all, what did it have to do with them? Roosevelt knew that although he was in a stronger position after the Pearl Harbor attack if there was to be an invasion of Europe, the American people still wouldn't accept their armies being led by a foreign general. Churchill understood this and could accept it in the greater scheme of things. If having an American in overall command was the price that had to be paid for the military focus of both countries to remain on Europe, then he was prepared to pay it. He also pledged to send more British and Commonwealth troops to fight in the Pacific and Burma, but first he needed Nazi Germany to be defeated, and once that was achieved he could then focus his efforts against the Japanese, regain Singapore and help America as best he could in the Pacific.

Supreme Headquarters Allied Expeditionary Force, more commonly known as SHAEF, was set up in December 1943 at Camp Griffiss, Bushy Park, Teddington, London, and remained there until 14 July 1945. During its existence it only ever had one commander: Eisenhower, the Supreme Allied Commander.

Below is the exact wording of a letter that was issued on behalf of General Eisenhower to all military personnel who took part in Operation Overlord:

Supreme Headquarters
Allied Expeditionary Force

Soldiers, Sailors and Airmen of the Allied Expeditionary Force!

You are about to embark on the Great Crusade, toward which we have striven these many months. The eyes of the world are upon you. The hopes and prayers of liberty loving people everywhere march with you. In company with our brave Allies and brothers in arms on other Fronts, you will bring about the destruction of the German war machine, the elimination of Nazi tyranny over the oppressed peoples of Europe, and security for ourselves in a free world.

Your task will not be an easy one. Your enemy is well trained, well equipped and battle-hardened. He will fight savagely.

But this is the year 1944! Much has happened since the Nazi triumphs of 1940-41. The United Nations have inflicted upon the Germans great defeats, in open battle, man-to-man. Our air offensive has seriously reduced their strength in the air and their capacity to wage war on the ground. Our Home Fronts have given us an overwhelming superiority in weapons and munitions of war, and placed at our disposal great reserves of trained fighting men. The tide has turned! The free men of the world are marching together to victory.

I have full confidence in your courage, devotion to duty, and skill in battle. We will accept nothing less than full victory.

Good luck! And let us all beseech the blessing of Almighty God upon this great and noble undertaking.

Dwight D. Eisenhower.

The operation was the brainchild of Lieutenant General Frederick E. Morgan, who was the Chief of Staff to the Supreme Allied Forces, and Major General Ray Barker.

Next in line to Eisenhower came the deputy supreme allied commander, Air Chief Marshal Sir Arthur Tedder. Under them were five ground commanders: Montgomery, who was in charge of the 21st Army Group, Lieutenant General Omar N. Bradley, the man in charge of the 12th Army Group, Lieutenant General Jacob L. Devers, who led the 6th Army Group, Air Marshall Sir

Trafford Leigh-Mallory, who was the Commander of the Air Forces, and Admiral Sir Bertram Ramsay, who was the Naval Forces Commander.

It was noticeable that three of the commanders, including Eisenhower, were American, while the other four were British. Neither Canada nor France were represented as far as senior officers were concerned.

The First Allied Airborne Army, which also became part of SHAEF, but wasn't formed until 2 August 1944, came under the command of American officer Lieutenant Colonel Lewis H. Brereton and British officer General Richard Nelson Gale, the latter of whom had the rather unfortunate nickname of 'Windy'.

The 21st Army Group, under Montgomery, consisted of the British Second Army along with the First Canadian Army, and the latter also included a number of British and Polish troops. It had been set up in July 1943, with Operation Overlord and the invasion of German-occupied Europe its main purpose.

The British Second Army was under the command of Lieutenant General Miles Dempsey, who served in the British Army between 1915 and 1947. He had first seen action as a platoon commander during the Battle of Delville Wood in July 1916. The Second Army were heavily involved in the D-Day landings in Normandy on 6 June 1944.

The First Canadian Army had two different men in charge in 1944: Guy Granville Simonds, an Englishman by birth who had lived in Canada since he was 9; and, from March 1944, General Henry Duncan Graham Crerar, who had served in the Canadian Army since 1910.

The American 12th Army Group, which included the 1st, 3rd, 9th and 15th armies, played an important part during the D-Day landings. After the beachhead in Normandy had been secured, they formed the centre section of the Allied forces as they moved forward, forcing the Germans to spend the following year on the retreat.

The American 6th Army Group included the French First Army and the 7th US Army and was under the command of Lieutenant General Jacob L. Devers.

By 6 June 1944, Eisenhower was still the Supreme Allied Commander, with Arthur Tedder as the deputy. Montgomery was in charge of all Allied ground forces, Trafford Leigh-Mallory was in charge of all air operations, and Bertram Ramsay was the Naval commander-in-chief.

Ramsay had already had an extraordinary war. He had actually retired from the Royal Navy in 1938, having served for forty years, but had then returned at the personal request of Churchill, and was promoted to the rank of vice admiral. His first job was as commander-in-chief, Dover. This involved the security of Allied military vessels making their way across the Channel to stop German submarines passing through the straits of Dover and to prevent German naval attacks along the south coast of England. In May 1940 he was responsible for Operation Dynamo, the rescue of 338,226 troops from Dunkirk. His headquarters for Dynamo were in the underground tunnels beneath Dover Castle. I am in absolutely no doubt whatsoever that if Dynamo had failed, the war would have been lost then and there.

Operation Torch, which was the Allied invasion of North Africa between 8 and 16 November 1942, saw Ramsay in the position of naval commander. In 1943, Ramsay was involved Operation Husky, which was the Allied invasion of Sicily where he had to prepare the amphibious landing. As part of Overlord he commanded possibly the biggest fleet in military history when he was in charge of some 7,000 vessels of both the Royal and Merchant navies, taking men and equipment to the beaches of Normandy. Sadly, Ramsay didn't survive the war. He was killed on 2 January 1945 in an air crash on his way to a meeting with Montgomery.

The battle group that would set off for Normandy would consist of 1,212 warships, 4,126 landing craft, 1,600 merchant and other designated ships, 11,500 aircraft, 3,500 gliders, and an army of 3,500,000, of whom about 150,000 landed on the first day. Of these there were an estimated 10,249 casualties, 2,500 of whom were killed. The Americans suffered the most with 6,603 casualties. Britain was next with 2,700 and finally the Canadians with 946.

Next was Operation Pointblank, a combined Allied bombing offensive by RAF Bomber Command and the United States 8th Air Force, whose objective was to bomb specific targets such as aircraft factories, and disrupt and destroy German fighter aircraft. Without Allied air supremacy over northern France, it would have been almost suicidal to conduct an amphibious invasion. British and American aircraft bombed German facilities day and night. The RAF concentrated on night-time attacks on large industrial areas, while the USAAF carried out daytime, precision bombing of specific targets, which some classed as the more dangerous. The Messerschmitt BF-109 factory in Regensburg and a large oil refinery in the town were bombed by B-17s of the USAAF on 17 August 1943, as was the ball-bearing factory at Schweinfurt.

Chapter Three

Evacuation of the area around Slapton Sands

Slapton, in the South Hams area of Devon, is one of those places that hasn't changed that much over time. In 1901, the census shows that the quaint little village had a population of 527. Move forward one hundred years and by 2001, the population had dropped to 473, and by 2011, it had reduced even further, to just 434.

The village has a long history. It is mentioned in the Domesday Book that was completed by order of William the Conqueror in 1086, when it was referred to by the name of Sladone.

The village boasts two grade I listed buildings. The first is the Church of St James which dates from the late thirteenth or early fourteenth century; the other is the west tower of what was originally the Collegiate Chantry of St Mary, which was founded by Sir Guy de Bryan in around 1372.

Neither the village's history, nor its peace and tranquillity saved it when the nation needed its help in the Second World War. Slapton and the areas immediately surrounding it had, unfortunately for the people who lived and worked there, become a very important part of the war. The reason was that its beach and its immediate hinterland area bore a striking resemblance to an area on the coast of Normandy that on 6 June 1944 would be one of the designated landing areas for Operation Overlord: 'Utah Beach'.

Slapton 'Sands', was, it could be argued, a strange name to give to the town's nearly mile-long beach, because it was actually a combination of shingle and small red pebbles, with hardly a speck of sand in sight.

As might be expected of the rural and coastal areas of the South Hams area, life moved at a slower pace than in some of the bigger surrounding towns. This is how it had been for many hundreds of years, with much of the land being used for farming, some of the farms having been tended by generations of the same family. For many it was all they had known. It was a way of life, with the expectation and assumption that the eldest son of the family would take over the farm from his father when he passed away or became too old or infirm to run it himself.

Many of the homes in the area were cottages, which gave the villages and communities which they stood in a picturesque, postcard appearance.

Slapton was a vision of peace and tranquillity where time had almost stood still, crime was limited to the odd case of drunkenness or poaching, the church was the focal point of the community, a place where everybody knew each other, and secrets were hard to keep.

Slapton, or rather its immediate coastline, became famous for the landing craft that came crashing ashore on its beaches in the war, but this wasn't the first time the beaches had been popular for the landing of boats. The seclusion of the area had been recognised long ago: besides local fishermen bringing their catches ashore, smugglers also found it an excellent location to bring in their illicit goods to avoid paying the taxman. There were those who became quite well off as a result of their smuggling activities.

A phone call was received by the chairman of the Devon County Council, Sir John Daw, on 4 November 1943, informing him that under the Defence Regulations Act 1939, a small part of South Devon had to be evacuated so that it could be used for military purposes, and that the entire population and their belongings, along with any livestock or crops, needed to be completely removed by 20 December 1943.

This was no mean feat as it meant that in just over six weeks some 3,000 people from about 750 homes, farms, shops and pubs that made up the villages in the prescribed area, all had to be moved out. There were no exceptions and no rights of appeal. The decision had been made, and that was the end of the matter.

The authorities had made the decision well in advance of actually announcing it, but they were in something of a quandary with the timing. They knew that it was not going to be possible to keep the secret no matter how cooperative the people concerned were. The longer it took to evacuate, the more it was going to come to the attention of people who didn't need to know about it. That being said, it was always going to be hard to keep it a secret. Not only were people moved out, but tens of thousands of American servicemen were moved in, barbed wire was placed all around the perimeter of the restricted area, and there were armed guards at strategic points making sure that nobody got in who didn't have official permission to be there. The more important issue was ensuring that nobody managed to work out what the *real* reason behind the training was.

The designated area requisitioned by the War Office included the eight villages of Blackawton, Chillington, East Allington, Torcross, Sherford, Slapton, Stokenham, and Strete. Beaches not just in Devon but all along the south coast had been off limits to members of the public since the beginning of the war. Holiday makers and families frolicking on the beach had been replaced with mines, barbed wire, defensive obstacles, and keep out signs, such was the belief that the Germans intended an invasion of England somewhere along the south coast.

On Friday, 12 November 1943, two hastily arranged meetings took place, one in the afternoon at East Allington Church, and another that evening at Stokenham Church. Both were chaired by Earl Fortescue MC, the Lord Lieutenant of Devon, who was hoping for a big turnout despite the rain. The next day another meeting took place at Blackawton Church, chaired by Sir John Daw. The purpose of these meetings was to inform the residents of the area what was going on, why they needed to be moved out, by when they had to be gone, and how they were going to move their belongings, livestock, and even crops – because everything had to go.

Obviously, these were difficult times. There was a war on, some of the men from the affected villages had enlisted in the armed forces and were away fighting. Some of the residents were elderly and not very mobile. Where would they go, where would they live, how long would they have to stay there for? Would their homes still be standing when, and if, they eventually returned? Would they receive compensation for their enforced move? All of these were valid questions Sir John Daw and Earl Fortescue did their best to answer. The authorities understood that the upheaval would be upsetting, but they also knew that it was a necessary evil for the greater good. If it allowed American soldiers to be able to move in and train so their assault on the beaches of Normandy would be successful, most people would no doubt agree that it was a price worth paying.

Notices were put up throughout the district which contained information and dates in regard to the evacuation:

NOTICE

The public are reminded that requisition took effect from November 16th, from which date compensation is calculated. They will not, except for special reason, be disturbed in their possession until December 21st, but from that date the Admiralty may at any time and without notice enforce their right to immediate possession. It is therefore essential that EVERY PERSON SHOULD LEAVE THE AREA BY DECEMBER 20th.

On December 20th the supply of electricity in the area will cease. The present measures for supplying food will not be continued but will be replaced by arrangements of a purely emergency character. The Police stations will be closing during the present week.

THE INFORMATION CENTRES will remain OPEN on SUNDAY, DECEMBER 19th. They will be CLOSED from DECEMBER 21st, but officers will be present at BLACKAWTON to deal with urgent matters.

The telephone numbers of the information centres are;

BLACKAWTON - Blackawton 47 and 49.

STOKENHAM – Kingsbridge 2386 and 2387.

As from December 21st, all compensation matters will be dealt with by the Admiralty at DITTISHAM COURT HOTEL. (Tel. Dittisham 31).

Transport must now be taken on the date allotted except in case of serious illness. All cases of illness which may affect removal must be immediately reported to the Information Centres.

Signed K G HARPER
MINISTRY OF HOME SECURITY.

The information centres proved helpful and were open most days from 8.30 am until 5 pm, and sometimes as late 7 pm, such was their desire to be as helpful as possible.

No expense was spared by the authorities to help everybody move out of their homes on time. Help came in all shapes and sizes. The American military provided men and trucks to help the villagers remove their belongings, along with elements of the Home Guard, Civil Defence, Women's Volunteer Service, members of the local VAD units, and other volunteer organisations. A combination of cars, trucks, lorries and even a steam engine and wooden carriages were used. Assistance was also provided to residents if they wished to view a property they were looking at temporarily renting, or to conduct any other business for that matter which was connected to their evacuation. This came in the form of being provided with a car and a driver, usually from the Women's Volunteer Service, and sufficient petrol for the round trip, free of charge. This was at a time when petrol for private use had been withdrawn completely and large cars were confiscated and converted for use as vans or ambulances.

A large number of lorries were also needed to move each household's belongings. These came from all over the country, or put another way, from wherever they could be found and commandeered. There was no way of knowing exactly how long evacuating each home was going to take, especially the farms, of which there were many in the restricted area. With them, it wasn't just the items in the family home that had to be moved: machinery, livestock and everything in the outbuildings and barns had to be moved too. Even the crops.

Overcrowding was becoming a problem in the south-west during the Second World War. Some of the larger towns such as Plymouth, Weymouth, Exeter and Torquay had been badly bombed by the Luftwaffe, making them unsafe places to be. Children and in some cases entire families were moved out to the country for their safety, but the problem quickly became where to put them all. Also, by the beginning of 1944 there were tens of thousands of American soldiers dotted around the south-west of England involved in training exercises. Most had been put up in specially designated army camps or already established military barracks, but some, usually those who held officer ranks, were billeted in private homes or hotels. Add to that another 3,000 individuals from some 750 families who also now needed somewhere to live for an unknown period of time, and that part of the country had become pretty well saturated as far as the amount of people it could cope with.

In the South Hams, most villages were reachable via narrow lanes that survived from a time when the largest vehicles that used them would have been horse and cart. Despite motor vehicles having become the new means of travel for most, the lanes were still as narrow as they had always been and were still no more than a dirt track or a leafy lane. Both track and lane had one thing in common: it wouldn't take much rain to turn either into a quagmire; and the evacuations were taking place in the middle of winter, making such conditions much more likely. If one truck met another coming in the opposite direction down one of these country lanes the only option was for one of them to stop, place the vehicle in reverse gear, and travel backwards, possibly for a long distance, until a suitable gap materialised for him to reverse into so the other driver could pass, the whole time hoping that he didn't skid off the road in to a nearby ditch.

Many of the drivers of these vehicles were not local men and could only find the properties they were going to by consulting the written directions with which they had been provided. After Dunkirk it was feared that a German invasion would quickly follow; to make it as difficult as possible for an enemy force, it was ordered that all road signs be removed to cause maximum confusion. It certainly confused the drivers of the lorries in the lanes of the South Hams. The situation was aggravated further still as the more people who were evacuated meant that there were fewer people to stop and ask for directions.

It can only be guessed what it must have been like for the elderly of the evacuated communities. For many, the homes they were leaving behind were the only ones they had ever lived in. The countryside was all they had ever known, and moving to a town, no matter how near or far away, might have just as well been on the other side of the world for the change it brought to their lives. For many it was the normality of their day-to-day existence which kept them going, walking the same routes and chatting with the same people every day.

Once the evacuation was complete, a number of officially approved photographers and surveyors where dispatched to the area so that proper accounts of what had been left behind could be comprehensively recorded and valued, so that once the Americans had left, it would be relatively easy to ensure that every property was in the same condition as when it had originally been handed over, and if there were any disputes concerning the condition of returned properties, they could be easily resolved.

As the last truck moved out, Slapton became like a ghost town. It was like a land-based version of the *Marie Celeste*.

Once the civilian population had moved out, the American soldiers moved in to begin their training. Slapton became a restricted military area where civilians were banned, and only those with special permits were allowed in. The troops wasted no time getting to work, and soon they had set up defensive positions, guard posts, erected barbed wire fencing, encampments for the troops, vehicles, fuel and munitions, and some of the taller buildings or those built on higher ground were used as observation points.

It was always going to be difficult to keep what was going in the area a secret, but people were still asked to keep quiet about what they had seen, heard and knew. Armed guards were placed around the perimeter of the restricted area while men, vehicles, equipment and food, were moved in under tight security.

It wasn't just Slapton where there were American troops. They were all over the West Country. Some were there to try out new weapons before they were judged suitable for use on the beaches of Normandy. For this reason, once they had been fired and used by the American soldiers, they were then used in exercises, many of which involved live firing, where bullets were fired over the heads of advancing troops, to try and make every step of their training as realistic as possible. Once these new weapons had been tried and tested during exercises, and found to be suitable, they would play a greater role in the months ahead and the final operation, which everybody was building up to, whether they knew it or not.

On the matter of evacuations of identified areas for military purposes, and despite not being part of the restricted military area of the South Hams in Devon, I feel it relevant to mention the villages of Tyneham in Dorset and Imber on Salisbury Plain in Wiltshire by way of a direct comparison.

Tyneham is situated on the Isle of Purbeck. Before the war it was one of Dorset's numerous quaint, picturesque villages and had a population of 225. The day that would change their lives forever was 17 November 1943, because this was the day that every home in the village received a letter from the War Office. It read as follows:

> *In order to give our troops the fullest opportunity to perfect their training in the use of modern weapons of war, the Army must have an area of land particularly suited to their special needs and in which they can use live shells. For this reason, you will realise the chosen area must be cleared of all civilians.*
>
> *The most careful search has been made to find an area suitable for the Army's purpose and which, at the same time, will involve the smallest number of persons and property. The area decided on, after the most careful study and consultation between all the Government Authorities concerned, lies roughly inside the square formed by East Lulworth, East Stoke, East Holme, and Kimmeridge Bay, which includes your property.*
>
> *It is regretted that in the National Interest, it is necessary to move you from your home, and everything possible will be done to help you, both by payment of compensation, and by finding other accommodation for you if you are unable to do so yourself.*
>
> *The date on which the military will take over this area is the 19th December next, and all civilians must be out of the area by that date.*
>
> *A special office will be opened at Westport house, WAREHAM, on Wednesday 17 November 1943, and you will be able to get advice between the hours of 10 am and 7 pm from there on your personal problems and difficulties. Any letters should be sent to that address also for the present.*
>
> *The Government appreciate that this is no small sacrifice which you are asked to make, but they are sure that you will give this further help, towards winning the war, with a good heart.*
>
> *C H MILLER*
>
> *Major-General i/c Administration*
>
> *Southern Command.*

Nearly all of the villagers who left were rehomed in newly built houses in nearby Wareham, although they were all promised that they would be able to return home once the war was over. Some residents liked their new homes and decided to stay there. Others wanted to return to their homes in Tyneham, but all such hope of that happening was finally quashed in 1948 when a compulsory order was placed on the area which meant that it remained under the control of the Ministry of Defence who wished to use it for gunnery ranges. Seventy years later the area is still used for the same purpose. Only remnants of the village survive, in the shape of derelict buildings that were once full of life.

Sadly for the residents of Tyneham, in 1943 they were in the wrong place at the wrong time. There was a war on, which had to be won at all costs. The village was not far from Bovington where tanks for the army were developed and built. The army needed somewhere for the tanks to be tested, Tyneham fitted the bill too nicely.

Imber, which boasts the beautiful thirteenth-century Church of St Giles, is situated on Salisbury Plain in Wiltshire. On 17 December 1943 the village ceased to exist. Its 152 residents were informed on 1 November that they had to leave, which gave them just forty-seven days to pack up all of their belongings and move out.

They were called to a meeting at the schoolroom and told that the reason they had to leave was that American forces would be using the village to practise street fighting. It later transpired that this was not the case. In the early 1970s the Defence Land Committee was tasked with looking at which land owned by the Ministry of Defence needed to be retained and which could be sold off. Richard Madigan, who had been a British soldier during the Second World War, was one of those who had assisted in the evacuation of Imber's residents and whose other duties had involved looking after the village and keeping it in good repair for when the residents returned after the war. The real reason for the evictions was that Imber was near proposed artillery shell impact areas. Despite a public inquiry, the residents of Imber were never allowed to return to their homes and the 'village' remained in the hands of the Ministry of Defence.

Imber was in a slightly different situation to both Tyneham and Slapton Sands, as the land the village sat on was actually owned by the War Office, who had been buying up farms and land in the area since the 1920s. This was at a time of a depression in the agricultural industry, and with the military prepared to offer favourable prices, there were not many who were unhappy to sell up, especially as most were then allowed to remain and pay rent for the land which they had once owned. The only area of land in Imber that was not owned by the War Office was that which included St Giles's Church, the vicarage, the chapel, the schoolroom and the Bell Inn.

On 13 April 1942 Imber was the scene of a tragic wartime accident which resulted in the deaths of 25 soldiers, with a further 71 wounded. An RAF Hurricane was taking part in a firepower demonstration when, inexplicably, the pilot fired on a crowd of military spectators who were on hand to witness the day's proceedings. Inclement weather and pilot error were blamed for the tragedy.

Six Hurricanes from No.175 Squadron and six Spitfires from No.234 Squadron were taking part in a demonstration of tactical airpower, which was a dress rehearsal for a planned visit by Winston Churchill and the Chief of Staff of the United States Army, General George Marshall. The twelve aircraft were tasked with attacking a number of armoured vehicles, mocked up tanks and dummies representing enemy soldiers.

A brief official statement was issued the following day by the War Office and the Air Ministry:

> *During combined exercises yesterday, in Southern England, there was an unfortunate accident in which a number of soldiers, including some members of the Home Guard, were killed, and others injured. The next of kin have been informed.*

The pilot of the aircraft had to give evidence to a court of inquiry. Sergeant William McLachlan, aged 21, told the court that he lost sight of the aircraft he was following and mistook the spectators for dummies, believing they were part of the exercise. It was found that he had made an error of judgement, with the hazy weather which prevailed at the time deemed to have contributed to the incident.

The official finding at the subsequent inquest held at nearby Warminster was misadventure and that the deaths were caused by gunshot wounds. The coroner took the unusual step of pointing out that, despite rumours, Sergeant McLachlan was British and not American. Why he decided to highlight that point is unclear. Maybe he was pressured into it by higher authorities who were concerned of the damage that a friendly fire incident might cause politically and in the eyes of the British public. McLachlan was in fact an American national who had enlisted in the Royal Canadian Air Force.

St Giles's Church, which is in full working order and is open to the public on certain days of the year, is unique as it is the only church in Great Britain which is surrounded by a ten foot high metal mesh fence, topped off with two feet of barbed wire. There are some people who are allowed to return permanently to Imber: those who once lived in the village and who have died are allowed back to be buried in the grounds of St Giles's.

Chapter Four

The Return of the evacuees

Although news of what large numbers of American soldiers were doing in the Devon countryside between January and May 1944 was kept a secret from the general public, once the D-Day landings had taken place the story of what they were really up to didn't take long to emerge. By late July 1944, newspaper articles told of what had been going on in the area of Slapton Sands and the surrounding area during its occupation by the American Army.

A number of roads were badly damaged by the heavy American military vehicles that were brought into the area to take part in what had been code-named Exercise Tiger. Many of the hedges and stone walls that had adorned either side of the roads had been damaged or knocked down altogether. Gardens were particularly noticeable as many of their lawns were knee high with grass. A field awash with poppies might have been a glorious sight to a passer-by who could appreciate its colour and serenity, but to the returning farmer, not so much.

There wasn't an animal of any description to be seen grazing in any of the fields, although in the driveway of one of the temporarily abandoned homes sat a well fed, healthy looking rabbit, peacefully contemplating his surroundings. Besides 'Roger' the rabbit, the only other visible sign of animal life was a quartet of young swans and a small number of water fowl, happily swimming round in the unruffled waters of Slapton Ley.

Even though, by this time, nobody had yet returned to their homes, workers from the GPO were already at work in the area. It was Saturday, 15 July 1944, when those who had been evacuated heard the news that most of them had been waiting for: that soon they would be able to return to their homes and get back to their normal lives.

Miss Brooking ran her own business in Chillington, where her family had lived for many years and where she was born. While she had been away she had been living most of the time at nearby Aveton Gifford and she was overjoyed to hear the news of the imminent return home on her wireless set. She was also glad that the sacrifice that she and her neighbours made had not been in vain and that the Normandy landings had been a success.

Mr Clements of Stokenham was a builder and ran his business out of Chillington. When they were evacuated, his machinery had to be placed in storage for the months they were away. Mr and Mrs Clements would watch for the red flag which indicated when live firing was taking place in the nearby fields. After not seeing the flag for a few weeks they were hopeful that whatever was going on had come to an end and they would soon be able to return to their home. But their hopes were short-lived when they saw black troops entering the restricted area and realised they would be waiting longer.

Mrs Curzen's husband was a butcher, and although many of his regular customers had, like him, been moved elsewhere, he had managed to keep his business going. But they were both looking forward to the day that they would be able to move back to their home.

Early August 1944 saw fuchsias in full bloom in the evacuated area of South Hams and the empty cottages would not have to wait long for their former occupants to return.

At a press conference that was held at Kingsbridge Urban Council Chambers on 2 August 1944, the task that needed to be done before the residents could return to their homes was explained before representatives were taken on a tour of the area. Mr G.C.N. Mackarness, the information officer for the south-west region, presided, while a statement was read out by Mr K.G. Harper, who represented the Regional Commissioner, General Sir Hugh Elles.

Mr Mackarness spoke highly of the way in which the people handled the evacuation. Many, he said, had lived in the area a long time and it meant a lot for them to have to leave. One of the first things that some of them asked was, what state their properties were going to be in on their return. It was obvious to most who had been evacuated that there would be damage to some if not all of their properties; it was just a question of how much.

A surprise to Mr Mackarness was that some of those residents who were allowed to return to their homes did not wish to. This was because while they had been living elsewhere they had for the first time experienced the wonders of running water and electricity and did not want to return to having to pump water from a well and using oil lamps to light their homes.

One farmer said he had no desire to return to his bombed-out farm and surrounding fields as he had no way of knowing how long it would take to make his property safe again.

Mr Harper had taken up residence in the area and was available to answer questions about how long it was going to take for people to return to their homes. The efforts to repair all of the damaged properties, roads, pavements and hedgerows, had been unceasing. There had been searches to ensure discarded munitions had been collected, although this aspect of the work had not been thoroughly completed and required more time. One thousand American soldiers had been allocated to the area to assist in the clear up.

Mr Mackarness said he had been amazed at the American soldiers' good will and thoughtfulness. They had collected £6,000, which would be worth several hundred thousand at today's rate, to be given out to deserving cases that were somehow not covered by the available monies provided by government. He emphasised that the area was not yet officially open and that police permission was required to enter.

When the evacuation farms, some 7,000 tons of mangolds, 2,000 tons of hay, baled and graded, and a large quantity of livestock had been moved. These all had to be moved back. At the time, there were only two army lorries available, and it took more than two weeks to do this.

The number of houses that had been destroyed was minimal, and the number of severely damaged houses was practically non-existent, except in Slapton and Strete. Elsewhere the damage was mostly superficial, such as broken or cracked windows, and doors that had been smashed or blown off their hinges. Farm houses, for some reason, had in the main escaped. Farm land had not however, the ground either churned up by tanks or other heavy vehicles, or from artillery rounds which had left behind many craters, some of which had filled with water.

Mr Mackarness further explained that the Devon Agricultural War Committee was responsible for some of the rehabilitation of the area such as gates and fencing, while the government, through the Ministry of Works and other different channels, would be responsible for the restoration of everything else, and would also be responsible for co-ordinating the return of the residents.

Regardless of how quickly damaged properties were repaired, it wouldn't be until the authorities were satisfied that all explosives had been removed from the area that a certificate of clearance would be issued to allow the residents' return.

Mr Harper explained that the principle that had been adopted was to prioritise the restoration of farms and to get farmers back on their land as expediently as possible, for the benefit of the local community as well as the nation as a whole. The general wish of the farmers was not to be kept off their land until it had been fully restored to its previous condition, but to be admitted as soon as the farm houses were in order and the Admiralty Land Office had made a record of the state of them so that compensation could be dealt with fully. Recording of all of the damage thoroughly would prevent any rogue claims arising in the future.

The local farmers were really well looked after, even being provided with an additional labour force and machinery. In addition, another squad of men were in the area, available to be hired by farmers.

Labour and machinery were paid for by the farmers, who then received compensation based on the condition a farm had been in November and December 1943 when the evacuation took place compared with the condition it was in when the farmer returned.

Ordinary people were not forgotten when it came to being helped on their return. Reasonable expenses were met by the Admiralty. As soon as the villages were inhabitable again, every family was sent a letter informing them that they could return to their home. A printed note was included with each letter, with information about what help was available to them and a personal enquiry form for them to complete.

For those who owned a car or truck, petrol was made available enabling them to bring home their belongings, and for other necessary journeys in connection with their return, including visits to see their homes before they were allowed home. Vehicles that had been mothballed due to wartime restrictions could be provided with exemption certificates so that they could be used for the purpose.

Every household was provided, free of charge, with half a ton of coal, which was waiting for them on their return to their homes, while the Ministry of Fuel and Power took the necessary steps to see that there were sufficient coal reserves held in the Kingsbridge area to enable stocks to be built up.

Mr Harper said that the operation had thrown up some unexpected issues, such as elderly residents not being able to pack their belongings to bring them home. Where windows or doors had been broken, properties had been left open to the elements; in such cases there was a need to ensure that the insides were dry so that they were once again inhabitable. To this end Mr Harper had instructed that every home would be visited and inspected to ensure there were no dampness issues. Those found to be damp had coal fires set in the hearth. Much of this work had been carried out by the Women's Volunteer Service, for which Mr Harper was extremely grateful.

After Mr Harper and Mr Mackarness had finished what they had to say, and then dealt with questions from the attendant press, a vehicular tour of the restricted area was provided so that reporters could see for themselves the work that had been done so far, and what still needed doing to make the area inhabitable once again.

At the entrance to the restricted area the convoy stopped for a collective chat with Miss Ruth Friend. She and her father Edwin lived at Chillington. They were one of the last families to leave the area, moving out on the very last day. Even then they didn't move far. They took up residence at a cottage only a matter of yards away from the barbed wire barrier that separated the restricted military area from the outside world, and they couldn't wait to get back to their home.

At nearby Torcross the group met 68-year-old Mr Lewis Alfred Guest, who had been provided with an official pass so that he could visit his home at 6 Florence Cottages. He was well-known in the area as he worked as a coach driver. He told the reporters that his home was in a reasonable state of affairs, especially taking in to account what it had been used for, and as soon as he was let back in, he would quite easily be able to fix it and make it right again. Lewis Guest died in Plymouth in 1964 aged 88. Somewhat remarkably he was still living at the same address in Torcross. His wife Avice survived him.

Another person that the group of reporters bumped into in Torcross was Mr H. Sutton, also a bus driver. Before the evacuation he had been cultivating a couple of acres of land and rebuilding his house as well as working full-time on the buses. He was keen to return to his property so he could begin weeding.

It was reported on 22 September 1944 that some two hundred Italian co-operationists were assisting in the work of rehabilitation in the area repairing the roads. A further thirty were engaged in farm work, alongside twenty-five Land Girls and some Irish labourers. Italy had surrendered to the Americans on 23 September 1943 and then declared war on Germany on 13 October 1943. This did not mean the immediate release of Italian PoWs being held by the Allies, but their categorisation was changed and they became known as co-operators in what were termed Italian Service Units.

The village of East Allington was the first to be released from what had been designated a restricted military area. The soldiers had gone and the pretend fighting had come to an end, to be replaced by cats and dogs and young children playing in the fields which had previously been full of mines and other types of military hardware. A service was held in the parish church, where about one hundred residents heartily joined in the doxology.

Residents of Sherford, Blackawton and Chillington were fully released from the restricted military area by the end of September 1944. Parts of Torcross and Stokenham were the next places to be handed back, but the coastal road which ran across Slapton Ley could not be opened until the walls on the road that overlooked Blackpool Beach were repaired.

The building repairs took longer to complete than had at first been anticipated due to a shortage of labour. It was reported in the local newspapers on 21 October 1944 that repair work was still continuing in the South Hams.

It would be the best part of a year before all the displaced residents could return to their homes. At 11am on Sunday, 5 November 1944, the Bishop of Exeter, Dr C.E. Curzon, attended a thanksgiving service at the twelfth-century Church of St Michael and All Angels, the Blackawton parish church, to commemorate the return of parishioners to the village. The communion was given by the bishop, who also read the lessons. He was ably assisted by the Reverend W.J. Berman-Davies, who said, 'It is a real joy to be back again, and it is only right and proper for us to offer our thanks to God as an act of public worship.' The Reverend informed his returning congregation that it would be necessary to find a substantial sum of money for the restoration work on the church. That Sunday's collection was put towards the restoration fund. In his address, the Bishop assured the community that it had the thanks, admiration and sympathy of the entire nation for their understanding and compliance with the evacuation from their homes that had been thrust upon them:

> *Now you are back again you have the knowledge of what your sacrifice has meant. We know now that D-Day was made possible by the training our Allies had in this area. Your sacrifice saved many lives in Normandy, and the giving up of your homes and fields also made possible the speedier return home of many thousands of our fellow men in enemy occupied countries. Your sacrifice has meant their freedom.*
>
> *What has happened might serve to remind us of the truth that great events are decided and great victories won, not by men whose names are known throughout the world, but by the unknown and unadvertised loyalty of ordinary men and women to duty imposed upon them.*

The joy of moving back was tempered somewhat for the people of Blackawton when it was discovered that damage to their Parish Church had occurred during the time it was occupied by American soldiers. As they were the only individuals allowed in the area when it was used as a training ground, it wasn't too difficult to work out who the perpetrators were. The church's vestry window had been smashed to enable entry, the organ had been badly damaged, all of the church's forty-one oil lamps were missing, as were all of the altar ornaments, except the cross. Also missing were the Holy Communion cruets and wafer box, the altar linen, the burses and veils, the alms bags and the pulpit falls. Fortunately the ancient chancel screen had been taken to a place of safety during the occupation; now it had to be resurrected. The task of restoration was going to be lengthy and costly, estimated to be over £1,200.

On 17 February 1945 it was reported that a letter had been received from Major Terrill, president of the Commonwealth Exploration Corporation and also an officer of the Los Angeles National Guard, who wrote,

> *I rejoice to note that our American boys obtained their highly valuable training in the Blackawton parish district, but I am grieved to note the acts of sacrilege performed by some person or persons unknown in stealing the vestment and other essential furnishings from the church.*
>
> *I note the appeal of the vicar of Blackawton for £1,200 to replace things stolen, more than likely as souvenirs, and which ere this have found their way by devious channels to our country.*
>
> *I intend to lay the whole matter before the Bishop of Los Angeles Diocese (Protestant), Rt. Rev. Bertram Stevens, seeking his co-operation in raising the sum called for by the vicar of Blackawton to restore the organ and to re-erect the chancel screen and provide the funds to replace all the lamps and other items that were stolen.*
>
> *Any wanton destruction would not be condoned by the people of America, especially those who are born citizens of Great Britain and who have now become citizens of the USA, like myself.*
>
> *The vicar of St Pauls Church (Protestant) in San Diego, is also named Stevens, a native of Brixham, Devonshire. I will also enlist his aid.*

How spooky was that? The priest in San Diego had the same surname as the one in Blackawton and came from Brixham, not a stone's throw from the village. Major Terrill was born in Totnes where he spent the early years of his life before emigrating to America, settling down in Los Angeles. It was nice to see that the situation was taken seriously by the Americans.

Wednesday, 22 November 1944, saw the beginning of the Devon Quarter Sessions at Exeter. One of the cases before the Justices was outlined to the court by the prosecution solicitor Mr Pratt: 'It was a sheer case of pique and malice after having being dismissed from his employment,' said

Mr Pratt. The man in question was 30-year-old Cyril Victor Sedgeman, a farm labourer who had admitted setting fire to two hayricks and a straw rick at Blackawton. The ricks, Mr Pratt informed the court, were valued at £120, and were totally destroyed along with a tarpaulin valued at £12 and four gates worth £6. One of the ricks actually belonged to a neighbouring farmer, Mr Pratt explained, Sedgeman having set fire to it in the belief that it belonged to his late employer. Sedgeman had eight previous convictions, one of which resulted in him receiving a twelve month custodial sentence for setting fire to four straw ricks in 1941. On this occasion, the chairman of the bench passed a sentence of twenty months imprisonment. What compounded the situation was that the community was just starting to get back on its feet after returning to their homes. In summing up the chairman of the bench told Sedgeman, 'You have behaved in a mean and despicable way towards not one, but two troubled farmers.'

While the residents had been away, a plague of uninvited rats had chosen Blackawton as their new home. They had killed and eaten more than a dozen of Mrs Peeke's hens at Forder Farm and were suspected of stealing eggs. In one cottage, a child had left her doll on the kitchen table overnight, only to find it had been torn to pieces the next morning. Children's pet rabbits had also fallen foul of the rats after they had gnawed their way through the metal wire of the cages. At one of the farms a great deal of damage had been caused in one of the stores where potatoes were kept.

At Slapton, putty was eaten away round the window frames until Mr Northmore suggested painting over the top of the putty; miraculously this solved the problem. At Start Point Inn in Torcross the rats had managed to get into the thatched roof of the property.

The problem had become so bad that officials from the Ministry of Food in London had been hastily dispatched to the Devon village. Miss M. Neaves, a technical officer from the ministry, was in charge of the planning to rid the village of its rat infestation. On her arrival, she set up in the George Inn. She was assisted by Major G.P. O'Brien, who was the Ministry of Food's rodent inspector for South Devon, Mr H.G. Northmore, the rodent officer of Knightsbridge Rural Council, along with other officials from the Ministry of Food, including those from Exeter, Kingsbridge, Plymouth, and Totnes. They were joined by some villagers who pointed out the buildings where the rats had set up home and had begun to breed. Once the locations had been identified, food was put out for four days to get the rats used to eating at specific points, then, on the fifth day the food had poison added to it. Miss Neaves explained that great care was taken with the use of poison; householders were warned where it was laid and that they should keep their pets indoors and their animals safely locked up at night. Where this was not possible, a specific poison would be used that was only harmful to rats. A fine grain poison was used which caused the rats to die after a few hours or within two days, depending how much of the poison they had digested. Miss Neaves' team concentrated on dealing with the rats in the villages, while Captain H.W. Leonard, who was the War Agricultural Area Supervisor for Devon, and two teams of Land Girls, had been tasked with tackling the problems on the surrounding farms. Captain Leonard expected that it would take about ten days before they had finished their work.

In Blackawton, 10 March 1945 was a significant date as it saw the first wedding take place in the village since the return of its inhabitants. It was held at St Michaels and All Angels. The Bride was Miss Louisa Sylvia Lamble, the eldest daughter of the late Mr and Mrs H. Lamble of Chapel Street, Blackawton. She was a private in the Auxiliary Territorial Service. The groom was John Douglas Payne, a guardsman serving with the Grenadier Guards, the only son of Mr and Mrs J. Payne of 71 Perry Street, Northampton. The couple were married by Reverend Berman-Davies. In the absence of her dear departed father, Miss Lamble was given away by her uncle, Mr B.L. Way of Paignton. The bride looked resplendent in her wedding dress made of white taffeta, with an embroidered white veil, that was held in place by a coronet of orchids surmounted by a white dove. She carried a bouquet of red carnations. There were three bridesmaids, Miss Mary Lamble, the sister of the bride, Miss Pearl Payne, sister of the bridegroom, and Dorothy Way, the bride's cousin, all of whom wore pink dresses with blue taffeta edging. The reception was held in Blackawton.

Chapter Five

Exercise Tiger

xercise Tiger was part of the final rehearsals for the D–Day landings, involving American troops of assault force U who six weeks later were to land on Utah Beach. The chosen location for the exercise was Slapton Sands. By the time it was over, two incidents had resulted in the deaths of 749 American servicemen. The following is the wording of an American document about Exercise Tiger marked Top Secret and dated 19 April 1944:

SHAEF/23036/8/Trg
Subject: Exercise Tiger

1. *Exercise TIGER will involve the concentration, marshalling and embarkation of troops in the TORBAY – PLYMOUTH area, and a short movement by sea under the control of the US Navy, disembarkation with Naval and Air support at Slapton Sands, a beach assault using service ammunition, the securing of a beachhead and a rapid advance in land.*
2. *Major troop units are the VII Corps troops, 4th Infantry Division, the 101st and 82nd Airborne Divisions, 1st Engineer Special Brigade, Force "U" and supporting Air Force units.*
3. *During the period H-60 to H-45 minutes, fighter bombers attack inland targets on call from the 101st Airborne Division and medium bombers attack three targets along the beach. Additional targets will be bombed by both fighter bombers and medium bombers on call from ground units. Simulated missions will also be flown with the target areas marked by smoke pots.*
4. *Naval vessels fire upon beach obstacles from H-50 to H-hour, Smoke may be used during the latter part of the naval bombardment both from naval craft by 4.2" chemical mortars and at H-hour by planes, if weather conditions are favourable.*

Naval fire ceases at H-hour.

5. *The schedule of the exercise is as follows.*
22 April Move to marshalling areas commences.
D-Day 27 April 101st Airborne Division simulates landing.
Preparatory bombardment by air and navy.
Assault landing and advance of 4th Division.
28-29 April Advance of 4th Division & 101st Airborne Division continues.
82nd Airborne Division simulates landing, secure and holds objective.
(Exercise terminates on 29 April)
6. *Joining instructions will be issued later.*

W. R. Pierce
Colonel, G. S. C.
Chief, Training, Sub-Section

TOP SECRET
This paper must not be taken out of this Headquarters except as laid down in Paragraph 27, SHAEF Inter-Division Standing Security Regulations dated 9 February 1944.

Exercise Tiger began as planned on 22 April, and in essence this stage of the operation consisted of three days practising embarkation drills. As D-Day fast approached, Eisenhower wanted to make the operation as realistic and lifelike as it could possibly be. To achieve this, he made it a live firing operation, with artillery shells being dropped on the beaches ahead of the disembarking troops, and rifle and machine-gun fire that was aimed above the heads of the soldiers as they came ashore at Slapton Sands. He wanted his inexperienced troops hardened to real battlefield conditions, including the sights, sounds and smells that went with them, or at least as much as was possible in the circumstances. The troops would feel something of the confusion, the excitement, the fear and the uncertainty that they would experience in the real invasion. They would have to remain calm and controlled to be effective.

The Royal Navy had been tasked with providing protection for the exercise area at Lyme Bay with seven vessels. This included two destroyers, three Motor Torpedo Boats, two Motor Gun Boats, and because German high speed torpedo boats – E-boats – were known to patrol these waters from time to time, Royal Navy MTBs were also sent to patrol off Cherbourg in France, where the E-boats were based.

The first of the two incidents took place on the morning of 27 April 1944. The start time for the day's activities, or the first practice assault, had been earmarked for 0730 hours and would include a naval bombardment by vessels from the Force U Bombardment Group which consisted of British American and Dutch elements. Their formidable firepower would be directed onto the beaches at Slapton Sands at 0640 hours, fifty minutes before the troops were to land. The naval barrage that day came under the command of US Navy Rear Admiral Morton Lyndholm Deyo, a veteran of the First World War who had been in military service since 1907.

Admiral Moon's command ship, USS *Bayfield*, had arrived in the early hours of 27 April 1944 about 12 miles from the beaches of Slapton Sands out in Lyme Bay, along with Landing Craft Headquarters (LCH) 95, LCH-86, two other vessels of the US Navy and one from the British Navy. At about 0500, all of the landing craft she had on board had been lowered into the water ready to make their way to the beach. It was still dark, but only just, with dawn only minutes away.

The invasion of what had been designated Green Beach was due to begin at 0630 hours, or H-Hour, but the commander of the assault group contacted Admiral Moon to inform him that some of the LCIs had not yet arrived and suggested that H-Hour be delayed. After quickly assessing the situation, Moon agreed, and at 0625 hours ordered a delay of one hour.

Unfortunately, the decision to delay H-Hour was not received by all of the units, and they landed on the beaches at their originally allotted time. This was a live fire exercise, so there was no room for error. Shells landed on the beach at the same time as the soldiers and carnage resulted.

The second practice assault which took place on 28 April 1944, which was the T-4 convoy and consisted of seven Tank Landing Ships, or Landing Ships Tank, more routinely referred to as LSTs.

The LSTs were massive vessels, weighing in at about 5,500 tons, with some measuring over 400 feet in length, which meant that any change of speed or direction had to be planned well in advance. They had two load-carrying decks which could cater for nearly fifty military vehicles, including tanks. These vessels required crews of up to 169 officers and men and could cater for nearly 200 fully-laden combat-ready troops. The LSTs had eighteen guns mounted around her top decks. These included two twin 40mm guns, four single 40mm guns, and twelve single 20mm guns. Some of the vessels had different calibre guns, depending on how old they were. They were designed to land as far up on the beach as their weight would carry them; the bow then opened to allow the waiting vehicles to move down a hefty weighted ramp straight onto the beach where they were ready as an immediate support facility for the troops who came off with them.

Four of the vessels had sailed from Plymouth: USS LST-*515*, USS LST *496*, USS LST-*531* and USS LST-*58*; while a further four, USS LST-*499*, USS LST-*289*, USS LST-*511*, and USS LST-*507* left from Brixham Harbour. The convoy reached the area of Lyme Bay at about 0200 hours when one of the LSTs spotted two unidentified vessels approaching the T-4 convoy. Because of their close proximity, they were wrongly assumed to be two friendly ships. Who actually made that fateful assumption isn't known.

All of the vessels were, according to Admiralty charts, approximately 10 miles west-south-west of Portland Bill and 12 miles south of Burton Bradstock, which is actually about 45 miles away from Slapton Sands, when the attack by German E-boats began.

The first vessel to be attacked was USS LST-*507*. It was hit by a torpedo just after 0200 hours and then another about five minutes later. It didn't sink, but it burst into flames. Its men, now on board a badly damaged vessel, were now fired on by the machine guns of the same E-boats that were attacking them. Within thirty minutes it had to be abandoned, and by the break of dawn it had almost entirely sunk below the waves.

The USS LST-*507*, which had been launched on 16 November 1943, had on board elements of the 478th Amphibious Truck Company, the 557th Quartermaster Railhead Company, the 33rd Chemical Company, the 440th Engineer Company, the 1605th Engineer Map Depot Detachment, the 175th Signal Repair Company, the 3206th Quartermaster Service Company and the 3891st Quartermaster Truck Company, two ¼ ton trucks, one ¾ ton truck, thirteen 2½ ton trucks and twenty-two DUKWs. The final death toll was 202 US Army and Navy personnel.

DUKWs, more commonly referred to as Ducks, were wheeled amphibious landing craft. DUKW was not an acronym but a nomenclature of the company's manufacturing code.

The 3206th Quartermaster Service Company was nearly wiped out. At the start of the exercise they had a compliment of 251 officers and men out of which only 50 survived. The 557th Quartermaster Railhead Company lost 69 of its men. In the weeks after the E-boat attack, lost and damaged equipment was replaced and some of the units who had lost men had replacements arrive. The 3206th Quartermaster Service Company, because their losses had been so high, were replaced by the 363rd Quartermaster

Service Company, and the 557th Quartermaster Railhead Company was replaced by the 562nd Quartermaster Railhead Company.

An Interesting point about LST-*507* is that it wasn't struck from the Naval Register until 9 June 1944, three days after the beginning of the D-Day landings. Was that because of an administrative backlog of paperwork, or to hide the fact that it had been lost off Slapton Sands on 28 April 1944 and make it appear that it had actually been lost during the D-Day landings?

LST-*511* survived the attack and went on to take part in the D-Day landings, operating off Red Beach as part of the Omaha beachhead and acting as a hospital ship. She made fifty round trips between English ports and the beaches of Normandy conveying wounded men to safety. She came under the command of Lieutenant John Yacevich.

LST-*515*, despite being instructed not to attempt to pick up any survivors but to continue towards the beachhead, did in fact turn around and start looking for survivors. She also survived the E-boat attack and went on to participate in the D-Day landings at Omaha Beach. After the war, rather than being decommissioned, the LST-*515* was sent out to the Far East, where she remained until the end of 1952. She was eventually decommissioned in October 1955, but wasn't sold off, instead being recommissioned in August 1963 and renamed USS *Caddo Parish*. She was then used operationally by the United States Navy during the Vietnam War between 1965 and 1969 before being sold to the Philippine Navy in November 1969.

LST-*531* sank almost immediately after being struck by a torpedo fired by one of the E-boats, leaving little chance for the men aboard her to escape. A combined total of 736 soldiers and crew lost their lives. One of the officers from LST-*531* who was killed that day was Lieutenant John Henry Hill, of the United States Naval Reserve, whose home back in America was 10 Wendell Street, Cambridge, Boston.

LST-*58* survived the incident at Slapton Sands and went on to participate in the D-Day landings.

LST-*289* was badly damaged during Operation Tiger and the incident off Slapton Sands on 28 April 1944, resulting in her non-participation in the D-Day landings. After being repaired she was transferred to the Royal Navy in November 1944, where she remained in service until after the war. She was returned to the US Navy in October 1946.

LST-*496* was not damaged by any of the torpedoes fired in the early hours of 28 April 1944, but it did play a rather interesting part in the night's proceedings. During the attack some of the crew of LST-*496* fired at the fast-moving enemy craft, but in the darkness and confusion some of their machine-gun fire struck LST-*511*, wounding eighteen of her crew. She took part in the Normandy landings and there is a photograph of LST-*496* unloading her cargo of tanks and other military vehicles on to the Omaha beaches. Sadly she was sunk off Omaha beach on 11 June 1944 by mines.

LST-*499* survived the E-boat attack and went on to participate in the Normandy landings on 6 June 1944. She was sunk by enemy action on 8 June 1944.

The daring opportunist attack by the E-boats had caused a considerable amount of panic amongst the planners of the invasion of Europe, for three reasons.

They needed to prevent news of the incident and the subsequent fatalities from becoming public knowledge. There were more than 30,000 American servicemen who had taken part in the exercise, 946 of whom who had been killed, and their bodies, most of which had been recovered, required burying, and those wounded needed hospital treatment. There must have been many local residents living along the coastline where the incident took place who had heard the noise of the firing and explosions and seen the flames of the burning LST-*507*. To keep all of those involved from talking about what they had seen, heard, or experienced could not have been easy.

Not all the bodies of those killed had been recovered, which was a massive problem for the Allies. Ten of the officers reported missing were classed as 'Bigot level', meaning their security clearance was above top secret and they had intimate knowledge of the D-Day plans. It only needed one of these men to have been pulled from the waters of the Channel by the escaping German E-boats and taken prisoner for the D-Day plans to have been put in imminent danger of unravelling before their eyes. This was possibly one of the rare occasions in the war when senior Allied officers were hoping that some of their own men were dead rather than alive.

Two ships of the Royal Navy had been assigned to protect the convoy from enemy vessels. One of them, HMS *Scimitar*, a destroyer which had been in service with the Royal Navy as far back as twenty-six years earlier during the First World War, had suffered significant structural damage after having been in a collision with one of the American LSTs and had returned to Plymouth for repairs.

British naval headquarters and the American LSTs were working on different radio frequencies, which by today's standards is an elementary mistake. In today's world of organising either an operation or exercise, one of the first points to be discussed, if not the first, would be communications. Because of this oversight, the Americans were not aware that HMS *Scimitar* had left the convoy and returned to Plymouth. Her replacement, HMS *Saladin*, had been dispatched but did not arrive before the E-boats had carried out their attack. This left only HMS *Azalea* to protect the LSTs the best she could.

Azalea had received a radio message from naval headquarters that there were E-boats in the area, but sadly none of the escorted LSTs had received the same message, and the *Azalea,* possibly believing that they had, did not pass the message on to them.

Despite the Royal Navy having deployed MTBs to patrol off Cherbourg where the E-boats of the *Kriegsmarine* were based, the E-boats somehow bypassed them, made their way across the Channel managing to avoid HMS *Azalea*, and bypassed a line of other defending British vessels laid out across the vast opening of Lyme Bay, before carrying out their attack on the unsuspecting American LSTs.

MTB 701 of the Royal Navy's 63rd Motor Torpedo Boat Flotilla had been on patrol off the Channel Islands between the morning of the 24th and the morning of the 27th April 1944, when it returned to its base at the harbour at Portland Bill.

An article appeared in *Dorset Life* Magazine in May 2009 written by Rodney Legg under the heading 'Massacre at Slapton Sands – the Great Portland cover-up'. It told of Leading Telegraphist Nigel Cresswell and Able Seaman Torpedoman Wood who were serving with the Royal Navy's 63rd Motor Torpedo Boat Flotilla. Just after 7am on the morning of 28 April 1944, on what was a bright sunny spring day, they arrived in Lyme Bay where they saw hundreds of bodies floating in the water, including the bodies of soldiers dressed in British Army khaki battledress and wearing the distinctive square red shoulder badge of the Royal Artillery.

According to the Commonwealth War Graves Commission website, there were 23 members of the Royal Artillery who were killed or died on 28 April 1944. Of these 13 were buried in India, 5 in Italy, 1 in Myanmar, 1 in Thailand, and 2 in the UK.

Of the two who were buried in the UK, one was 50-year-old Battery Quartermaster Sergeant (1407167) Reginald Page of the 142nd (The Royal North Devon Yeomanry) Field Regiment, Royal Artillery. He was a married man who lived with his wife Eileen in Newton Poppleford, where he is buried in the village's cemetery close to St Luke's Church on the south side of Sidmouth Road. Reginald had also served during the First World War.

Apparently members of the British Royal Artillery had been deployed on the American LSTs as Bofors gunners.

From such a tragedy, some good could have come, but only if lessons were learnt from it. The attack from the E-boats certainly highlighted problems with the exercise, which after all was attempting to make the conditions as real as if it were an actual live operation.

It is believed that a number of men died during Exercise Tiger because they were wearing their lifebelts incorrectly; some were also faulty. In fact, most of the casualties that died off Slapton Sands on 28 April 1944 did so from either hypothermia or drowning. The latter cause was compounded by two issues: firstly as already mentioned, the problem with life jackets, secondly because many men either jumped into or found themselves in the sea in full battledress which once wet through, dragged them under the waves.

The general alarm system on the LSTs was somewhat confusing. For whatever reason it was determined that not everybody needed to be informed of what constituted a general alarm, or what to do if it was sounded, which seems somewhat at odds with the edict of making the exercise as real as possible. Instead notices were posted around the vessels with instructions about what to do if the general alarm was sounded, and officers were instructed to inform their men of the correct procedure if such an instance should prevail. Whether they actually did so or not is not recorded.

On LST-*507* only two out of the six available lifeboats were lowered. Some of those that weren't, their release pins were bent. Out of the two that were lowered, one capsized due to being overcrowded with nearly 100 men. The boat had a maximum capacity of sixty.

It was noted that discipline on board was of a poor standard in the aftermath of being struck by the torpedo. In the main this was because the loudspeaker system on board had been incapacitated by the explosions, so it was not possible for audible instructions to be given or heard. This led in some cases to men panicking as they did not know what to do. There was uncertainty, with some men unclear as to whether the call to abandon ship had been given or not. Such was the panic, some men were reported to have wasted valuable time searching for their duffle bags. Some survivors reported that some of their own officers and NCOs panicked, which added to the confusion and uncertainty that had gripped some of the men.

One of the other elements which undoubtedly hadn't helped matters any was the sense of boredom and repetition with what they were doing, and had been repeatedly doing since January 1944. Many of the men had taken part in fifteen or so similar exercises. They just wanted to get on with the real thing, whatever that might be.

Another of the dead from that day was Seaman First Class, Edwin James Dobson. Although initially he was reported missing in action, he was one of those lost on 28 April 1944.

There has been much subsequent debate as to whether or not there had been a cover-up about the events of that day, but I don't believe that was the case. For sure, there had to be some secrecy surrounding the events of that day, because the biggest and possibly the most important Allied operation of the Second World War was just six weeks away. If it was postponed or cancelled because of what happened at Slapton Sands, it could have meant the continuation of the war for many years.

To get 135,000 men and all of their equipment into position, in seclusion along the south coast of England, in readiness for the invasion, was no mean feat, but the longer they were kept there, the more chance there was of their real intention being discovered. The plans for the invasion of Europe had been worked out and drawn up, the number of men, equipment, ammunition, aircraft, ships, tanks, trucks, artillery pieces and other military vehicles had been amassed and squeezed into place. The final piece of the jigsaw was its implementation. The longer they waited, the more chance there was of their intentions coming to the notice of Nazi Germany, which ultimately could have meant the deaths or capture of 150,000 American, British and Canadian young men on the beaches of Normandy.

Remember, the tragedy at Slapton Sands had, in part, taken place because a German reconnaissance aircraft had spotted what it thought was a possible convoy of merchant ships making its way along the south-west coast of Great Britain. E-boats sent across the Channel to locate and destroy them did not realise the true significance of what they had discovered nor what was their purpose.

Senior military officers involved in the planning of the operation have to take some of the blame, because of the communications aspect along with not ensuring that men knew how to wear their lifebelts and, to a certain degree, because of the decision to make it a live firing exercise.

The Royal Navy have to take some of the blame for the escorting issue, although it wasn't entirely down to them. All in all, it illustrates the difficulties of making a training exercise truly realistic.

One of the issues with the Exercise Tiger story is a lack of clarity on what really happened: how many men were actually killed and where they were buried. Most of the bodies of the American servicemen who died were taken to Portland where they were processed by the US Army's

605th Quartermaster Graves Registration Company. After the 605th's work was done, the bodies were taken by the 146th Quartermaster Truck Company by road to the Brookwood Military Cemetery in Surrey where American military personnel were buried at the time. It wasn't until August 1944 that US casualties were buried and commemorated at the Cambridge American Cemetery and Memorial which is between the villages of Coton and Madingley. It was estimated by the 605th Graves Registration Company and the 146th Truck Company that they had processed 'in the 'region of' 500 bodies – there is no exact number, just an approximate one – but burial records at Brookwood Cemetery only related to 268 graves.

I believe the reference to a cover-up relates to two separate aspects of the exercise. There was the friendly fire incident that occurred on 27 April 1944 when an undisclosed number of American soldiers were killed by friendly fire after a confusion over the start time of that day's training exercise. Shelling of the beach by the Royal Navy's HMS *Hawkins* was originally planned to begin at 0730 hours, but it was delayed by one hour until 0830. Unfortunately, this change in the start time of the exercise was incredibly not passed on, which meant that rather than the subsequent artillery fire landing ahead of the disembarking American troops, it landed when they were already on the beach. There has never be a definitive answer as to the number of men who were killed in that incident; estimates vary between 200 and 500. This aspect of Exercise Tiger has never officially been recognised, confirmed or admitted by the American government or military authorities. This seems somewhat strange, as America came clean about the E-boat incident way back in 1954, so why they wouldn't confirm or clarify this aspect of the disaster is not clear. What makes matters worse is that because of this stance nobody knows for sure where these men were buried. Maybe their deaths were conveniently wrapped up with the casualty figures for the D-Day landings in Normandy.

The other case of alleged 'cover-up' is in relation to the aftermath of the E-boat attack, when hundreds of survivors were taken to nearby hospitals for the treatment of burns and immersion.

One of these hospitals was the US Army Field Hospital at the 228th Camp Unit at Haydon Park near the town of Sherbournc, which first opened for business on 18 September 1943. The hospital's staff, including doctors, nurses and orderlies, who were all military personnel, had no prior knowledge of the arrival of the wounded men. They were told to treat them but not to ask any questions about how they sustained their injuries and warned that they would be placed before a military court martial if they dared discuss the incident with anybody.

By the time the hospital had closed in late 1945 it had treated about 22,000 patients, both Allied and German.

Less than a month earlier, on 29 March 1944, and somewhat ironically in the circumstances, it might be said, the Sherbourne Camp had suffered its own tragedy connected to training for the D-Day landings. Some twenty-nine American soldiers of C Company, 294th Engineer Combat Battalion were killed at the end of an anti-tank mine-laying exercise which involved the placing of a minefield within the confines of Sherbourne Park as part of their final training for the invasion of Normandy. Troops were in the process of recovering mines they had laid earlier that morning when the truck which had the already-collected mines on board accidentally rolled backwards over one of the live mines causing an explosion which set off the other mines in a massive explosion.

The incident resulted in the deaths of 29 members of C Company, 294th Engineer Combat Battalion.

Sergeant Donald J. Walsh
Technician 5th Class Francis X. Gallagher
Technician 5th Class Warren F. Rapp
Technician 5th Class Lawrence C. Sbaratta
Private 1st Class Francis J. Murphy
Private 1st Class Martin A. Norton
Private Charles W. Brinkofski
Private Robert M. Bucella
Private Edward D. Chiarieri
Private Anthony Cutrone
Private John P. Deevy
Private John W. Gadek
Private Robert Gladen Jr
Private George Gundy
Private Harry B. Hanschka
Private Joseph B. Henning
Private Leonard B. Kerr
Private Stephen E. Kosicrowski
Private Roger E. Kroecer
Private Leo A. Lyon
Private John J. McHugh

Private Thomas S. Nicol
Private Lucien P. Pessoz
Private Conrad Propp
Private Robert L. Ready
Private Anthony T. Russo
Private Andrew Ter Waakreek
Private Fred C. Tracey
Private Joseph J. Zanelli

Because of the hospital's close proximity to the restricted military area, the incident of 20 March 1944 was classed as 'locational sensitivity' and therefore was not reported in the news until well after the war had ended.

Chapter Six

Deception

Once the decision had been made to invade German-occupied Europe, it was always going to take a monumental effort to make it happen, and there was no guarantee that it would succeed. Before D-Day there had been acts of subterfuge, the spreading of false information, and deception, to put the Germans off the scent of where the real invasion, which they knew was coming, was going to take place. For some strange reason the Germans always thought it was going to take place in the Pas-de-Calais region. Perhaps this was because it was the shortest crossing point of the English Channel, which one might have thought made it just a little too obvious.

Part of the subterfuge included deploying the robust and direct speaking General George Patton and his 3rd Army Group to train in Scotland. He still hadn't been fully forgiven for the slapping incidents in August 1943 when, leading the 7th Army in Sicily, he slapped and verbally abused two American soldiers who he felt were malingerers and cowards; they were patients in the 93rd Evacuation Hospital suffering from what today is called 'post-traumatic stress disorder'. The second incident took place on 10 August 1943: Patton became so angry that he drew one of his ivory-handled pistols, causing the hospital's commanding officer, Colonel Donald E. Currier, to step in between Patton and 21-year-old Private Paul G. Bennett of C Battery, 17th Field Artillery Regiment.

These incidents caused Eisenhower a problem. Despite attempts at keeping the incidents 'in house', word leaked out to the press, who printed details of the two events which amongst some sections of the public caused anger and outrage. He had to decide whether to sack Patton or just reprimand him.

Eisenhower knew Patton's worth as a commander. His aggressive nature inspired his men to greatness, something that most other military leaders got nowhere near achieving. But Patton's erratic behaviour didn't always go down well with his colleagues, or politicians for that matter. A balance had to be struck.

Patton was informed by Eisenhower on 1 January 1944 that he was relieving him of his command of the 7th Army and sending him to England where he was to be put in charge of the 3rd Army Group, most of whom were inexperienced and had never been in battle before. Eisenhower then continued the games that went with keeping the Germans guessing where the invasion of Europe would be coming from by sending Patton on widely announced trips to different locations throughout the Mediterranean. His travels took him to Algiers, Tunis, Cairo, Corsica, Malta and Jerusalem. Most of Germany's commanders held Patton in very high regard and could not foresee any scenario where an invasion of Europe would take place without Patton taking a prominent role.

The overall codename for these deceptions was Operation Bodyguard, with Patton being used as part of Operation Fortitude, which was split into two. Operation Fortitude (North) included providing the German High Command with information from double-agents about a phantom army that was based in Edinburgh, which was intended to make them believe that an invasion would take place somewhere along the Norwegian coastline. The possibility that they might also be considering an attack in the area of Pas-de-Calais was codenamed Operation Fortitude (South). Both options involved General Patton and the fictitious First United States Army Group. The hope was that the Germans would move troops to both of these locations, using some of those who were either in the Normandy area or close by as support.

It was also hoped that the deception could be continued after the invasion on 6 June 1944 so that the invasion at Normandy would be viewed as no more than a diversionary attack and that the main invasion was still due to take place at the Pas-de-Calais.

The planning of Operation Fortitude was carried out by the clandestine body known as the London Controlling Section whose existence wasn't even admitted until 1969, but it was still down to the theatre commander, which in this case was Eisenhower, to implement the plan. This in turn was passed on to the 21st Army Group under the command of Montgomery. The officer in charge of his deception staff, Colonel David Strangeways, didn't like the plan and set about rewriting it, and it was his idea to set up the fictitious First United States Army Group. If the plan was to be effective, the Germans would need to believe that the First United States Army Group was not only real but represented the main Allied invasion army that was coming for them somewhere in the area of Calais, regardless of what they heard about the landings at Normandy.

To achieve this, different methods of deception were used, the best form of which was public presence – in the case of the First United States Army Group, having somebody associated with it seen in specific locations.

Use of double agents, who were ultimately controlled by the Allies, enabled the passing of false information on to German military intelligence. There were many double agents who worked for the British in this capacity, but one in particular makes interesting reading: Juan Pujol Garcia, who was Spanish, went by the codename of Garbo. Not only did he manage to convince the Germans that he had created a non-existent spy ring of twenty-seven agents, but they were so impressed with the information he provided they awarded him the Iron Cross. After the war, he was awarded an MBE by the British.

False and misleading radio traffic was broadcast between non-existent units, which would knowingly be picked up by the Germans.

To enhance the validity of non-existent units, fake equipment such as dummy aircraft, tanks, landing craft and even airfields, were all manufactured and strategically placed in relevant locations.

Diplomatic channels were used to spread leaks of misinformation, which it was hoped would be either picked up by the Germans or passed on to them by other countries.

The Germans now knew of two Allied Army Groups: the 21st Army Group under Montgomery and the non-existent 1st United States Army Group under Patton.

Just how successful Operation Fortitude had become at confusing the Germans, became apparent on 1 June 1944 when the Allies intercepted dispatches from the Japanese ambassador to Germany, Hiroshi Oshima. In them he reported that he had spoken with Hitler and had been told by him that he believed any invasion of Europe would take place via the Straits of Dover and that any movement in Norway, Brittany or Normandy would be nothing more than diversionary feints. Oshima also said that the largest number of German troops and equipment would be concentrated in vicinity of the Pas-de-Calais and not Normandy. Oshima's dispatches from Germany to his superiors in Tokyo had been intercepted by the British since early 1941 and had proved invaluable. One, dated 19 January 1942, was particularly incredible. Ribbentrop, the German Minister of Foreign Affairs between 1938 and 1945, agreed to furnish Oshima with daily intelligence reports of how the war was going, which he was free to share with Tokyo. This was a massive mistake for Germany, as everything that Ribbentrop told Oshima was also inadvertently passed on to the British. In another, in November 1943, Oshima sent a twenty-page report to Tokyo about a four-day trip he had been taken on by the Germans in which he was shown the defensive fortifications of the Atlantic Wall. His report included the location of every German army division, its number of men and their weaponry. He also wrote in detail about the locations of tank ditches and the armament of artillery turrets, especially those nearest to the beaches, units that had been held in reserve in a mobile capacity so that they could be moved quickly to any given location. This information greatly helped the planners working on the landings in Normandy.

Oshima also unwittingly provided valuable information to the Allies about how successful their bombing raids on specific targets in Germany were.

After the German surrender, Oshima, his wife and staff were arrested in Bad Gastein in Austria. They were taken to the United States where they were interrogated and then sent back to Japan in November 1945. As he was not handed over to the British, it can only be assumed that either British intelligence officers were present while he was being questioned, or that the Americans shared with their Allies what Oshima had told them.

His freedom was short-lived as he was arrested in Japan on 16 December 1945 and charged with conspiracy to commit war crimes. He was found guilty on 12 November 1948 and sentenced to life imprisonment but was released on parole in 1955 and granted clemency in 1958. He died in 1975 in Tokyo aged 89, having never known of the important role he played as an unwitting Allied informant between 1941 and 1945.

Chapter Seven

Other Slapton Sands News

On the evening of Tuesday, 23 March 1943, nine months before Slapton Sands was evacuated and turned into a restricted military area, a German aircraft was shot down over the village.

It was written about the following day in local newspapers, as best it could be under wartime reporting restrictions. It was just before dusk when reports came in that German aircraft were in the skies over two south-west coastal villages dropping bombs and firing their machine guns on the buildings and people below. Apart from some slight blast damage and holes in fields, the attack accomplished little.

One of the aircraft was subsequently hit by anti-aircraft fire and came down in flames at Slapton Sands. The pilot did not survive. The incident was confirmed in a joint communiqué by the Air Ministry and the Ministry of Home Security.

In April 1943 it was possible to rent a house in the Slapton Sands area. One such property was available fully furnished: 'Charming compact detached residence. Six bedrooms, bathroom, 3 recreational rooms, sitting in 1 acre of gardens.' There was electric lighting as well as heating. The house offered beautiful views, maximum sunshine, and was on a bus route. The rental price was £4 4s per week, which included the cost of the gardener's wages. It was offered for rent by Victor Newton & Co, Auctioneers of Dartmouth.

In early October 1943, less than two months before families were forcibly moved out of their homes, a property sold in Slapton Sands for £1,750. It was stone built with four bedrooms, two reception rooms, a large lounge, a bath, what was called a cook-on-heat stove, a large kitchen and modern drainage, set in four and a half acres of well-maintained gardens including a garage, orchard and greenhouse, in the setting of a picturesque valley.

An article in the *Western Morning News* dated 20 July 1944 provided its readers with a brief insight into what had happened to the roads, fields and buildings of the area that had been designated as a restricted military area for the first six months of 1944:

No smoke curls from the chimneys. No cat washing itself on the cottage footstep. No hen clucking in the backyard, and no sleek cattle grazing in the overgrown fields.

Not a sound disturbs the un-natural silence of the South Devon evacuation area which a couple of months earlier had been the scene of fierce mock battles by means of which our American Allies prepared themselves for the invasion of Normandy.

Roses cascade over the walls of the deserted homes, and fruit ripens unpicked and drops to the ground from bushes in gardens where nature has been allowed to run riot.

Badly scarred, but still lovely, is this rural area to which the inhabitants, who were bundled out bag and baggage last Christmas, have been told they may soon return. Miles of glass will be required to replace the shattered windows, few of which remain intact, and much clearing up and repair work will have to be done before the people, who are looking forward to it with joyous anticipation, will be able to return.

The article continued in a descriptive manner about the other after effects of the occupation of their homes and fields by the young and eager American soldiers.

Even though the Americans had been careful and considerate while in temporary control of the area, the damage was extensive in some places. The hills overlooking the east end of Slapton Sands had the appearance of the aftermath of a hurricane. Having come under heavy shellfire from the ships of the Royal Navy, many of the trees had been either splintered or destroyed. Many of the stone walls that separated the farmers' fields from the roadway had been obliterated as if they had never existed, while many of the houses at sea level had suffered from direct hits and toppled like skittles in a bowling alley. Roads and sand had been churned up by the passage of heavy vehicles, and there were the remnants of concrete roadblocks and pillboxes that had been destroyed by shells. The beach had been transformed into something more akin to a scrap yard, with broken-down vehicles and landing craft strewn along the water's edge.

What had once been a well-maintained thatched-roof on a prominent building in the village of Strete had been destroyed by fire, although rumours that an entire village had been put to the flame were untrue. Military authorities had been thoughtful enough to mark churches and chapels as Out of Bounds and their roofs were marked to make them visible to the sea, but one church at Slapton Sands still sustained considerable damage, appearing to have been struck by two shells, and in Stokenham the church had received some minor damage to its slated roof. Some picturesque cottages in Torcross and Chillington had sustained major damage. The good news was, all of the damage was to be repaired or replaced.

It was reported at a meeting of the Rural District Council in July 1944 that residents should be allowed back to their homes beginning on 15 September. This applied to Blackawton, East Allington, Slapton, Strete, Stoke Fleming, Sherford and Stokenham, although with there being very little left of Strete, the building used by the Women's Institute being an exception, it wasn't clear what the residents of the village would actually be going back to.

At that same meeting, a local clergyman said he had heard that in one of the villages a field had been used as a cemetery. The chairman was quick to state that that was entirely false, as were many of the stories that had been circulated relating to damage done to property in the training area, although how he was able to make such a definitive statement is unclear.

It was also noted that the County War Agricultural Executive Committee would assist with the rehabilitation of the farms and was setting up an office in the area for this purpose. The intention was to get as many of the area's farmers as possible back before the arrival of winter, and to this end the committee promised to help by providing labour and assisting with the ploughing of the fields, although it was necessary to ensure that the fields were safe from the lurking danger of unexploded ordnance before that could begin. A hostel would to be built for the farm labourers. It was expected that a number would be girls of the Women's Land Army.

By August 1944, although the secret of the South Hams was revealed, it contained one glaring omission. There was no mention whatsoever of the loss of the hundreds of American personnel during Operation Tiger on 27 and 28 April 1944. Maybe with the war still in full swing it was deemed by senior military figures that 'now was not the time'. The last thing needed was for morale to be negatively affected.

The *Illustrated London News* of 12 August 1944 included some interesting photographs. One was of the remains of what had once been a reinforced concrete pillbox on the beach at Slapton Sands. Another was of houses on the outskirts of Slapton Sands that had been damaged by naval gunfire during the training exercises. A third shows black American troops on a street in Sherford, one of the villages in the battle rehearsal area which consisted in total of some 25 to 30 square miles of land. Two of the soldiers are sweeping the narrow road, while a group of four white soldiers can been seen on the side of the road watching them. Between 1942 and 1945 about one million American servicemen were based in England, mainly in the south; of these, about 130,000 were black.

The accompanying article explained how for six months before D-Day, the American soldiers, who on 6 June 1944 would land on the beaches of Normandy, were engaged in 'realistic mimic warfare carried out across rich Devon agricultural land'. They were assisted by vessels of the Royal Navy who cooperated in a live bombardment of the beaches and the coastal belt immediately to the rear of this area. The 'battle area' included a two-mile stretch at Slapton Sands.

An article in the *Western Morning News* dated 25 August 1944 described how arrangements had been made for the transport of the returning residents. The Regional Transport Commissioner appointed an Advisory Committee under the chairmanship of Mr W.G. Jerwood and an office was opened at 11 Mill Street, Kingsbridge to deal with enquiries. The transport industry had played an important role when the evacuation took place, which had not been easy due to the inclement weather and the available number of hours of light. Now the time had come for the repatriation of the residents, and the transport industry was again looking forward to playing their part.

It was hoped that residents of Strete would be able to start returning to their homes by the beginning of December. Damage at Slapton was more extensive than some of the neighbouring villages, and it was expected that it would be longer before the residents there could move back home. Besides the damage to property and the fields, a number of artillery shells and other munitions had been discovered which understandably prolonged the time it took to make the area safe.

It was a long time before it was possible to declare the beach at Slapton Ley safe, mainly because of the danger from unexploded hidden mines that might have been on the waste ground on the shore side of the road; the area was thoroughly searched with mine detectors. It was a slow process, as all mines had to be located before the residents could be allowed back.

Thursday 16 November 1944 was the closing date of the competition to design the memorial which was being provided by the American military to say thank you to the people of the South Hams. One proposed location for the memorial was the coast road between Blackpool and Strete Gate, where the sea wall was still being repaired. A letter was sent to the editor of the *Western Morning News* which appeared in the paper dated 15 February 1945. It was written by a Mr Samuel T. Gillbard:

> *Sir,*
>
> *Since returning to Slapton I find nearly every resident of the village considers the erection of a monument in memory of the occupation by the American forces should have taken the form of a most necessary need for a shelter, so that the inhabitants could appreciate American generosity.*
>
> *The American mind certainly has something more serviceable to offer us.*

The tragic deaths of two boys occurred at Slapton Ley on Wednesday, 7 March 1945. The inquest into their deaths took place at Kingsbridge on the 12th. Having heard the evidence, the coroner, Mr G. Windeatt, reached a verdict of 'Death by accidental drowning'.

The two boys were 16-year-old Claude Edward Powlesland, son of William Henry Powlesland, a baker of Ley View House, Torcross and of Loddiswell, and 17-year-old Herbert Reginald Bowles, son of Herbert Arthur Bowles, an agricultural worker of Brook Street, Slapton. Both of the boys were bakers' assistants.

Mr Powlesland told the inquest that the boys had gone to Lower Farm, Slapton, on the day of their deaths, where he saw his son nailing a square piece of timber on a pole, and thought it was for target practice. Eventually he saw the same pole with a similar piece of wood at either end, which had been formed in to a paddle.

During the afternoon, his son and Bowles went to Torcross to fetch milk churns, which is also where a 12-bore double-barrel shotgun with cartridges was kept. When he next saw the boys at about 2 o'clock the same afternoon, back in Slapton, they did not have the shotgun. When it got dark and the boys had not returned home, he got anxious and, along with Mr Bowles, the police and other local men who had volunteered to join them, he went to look for them. They carried on the search until 2 o'clock in the morning, by which time they had found no trace of the boys. At daybreak the search was resumed and a punt was found waterlogged in Slapton Ley. The shotgun was lying in the bottom of the boat, with the paddles found nearby.

Police Sergeant A. Milford, from Strete, told the inquest that about twenty men from Slapton village had joined the search. One of the volunteers had been a Mr William Burgoyne. He obtained a pair of braces which had belonged to Claude Powlesland and managed to trace the route which the boys took down to the Ley. He had used a divining rod of black whalebone. In the boat Mr Burgoyne indicated that he had received signs that the body of the Powlesland boy was in deep water some distance from the shore. The Ley was dragged with equipment brought from Beesands and the bodies of the boys were found in the early evening. The coroner said he had never seen nor heard of such power and ability that Mr Burgoyne undoubtedly possessed. He said that if needed Mr Burgoyne should provide his powers to assist the police, or anyone else in similar circumstances in the future.

On 7 July 1945 granite obelisk was unveiled on Slapton Sands to commemorate the operation and express the Americans' appreciation. There was a gathering of some 500 people to witness the unveiling of the memorial. The ceremony commenced with a prayer offered by Lieutenant Commander E.H.S. Chander of the US Naval Reserve, a Navy chaplain from Plymouth. Mr R.W. Prowse, Chairman of the Kingsbridge Rural Council, told what had happened at Slapton before and during the evacuation period.

Captain Ralph B. Hunt, Commander of US Navy amphibious bases in the UK, said, 'What happened on the Normandy beaches on June 6th 1944, and its following great success which led to victory in Europe, was acted out with the greatest thoroughness, not once, but many times on this site, right here at Slapton Sands.'

General John Lee, Commander of US Army Service Forces, said that when Americans travelling in England saw the monument, he hoped they would appreciate what the area and the people meant to them as it did to the United States Army.

The monument was accepted on behalf of the people of the South Hams by Sir John Daw, the Chairman of Devon County Council.

Earl Fortescue, the Lord Lieutenant of Devon, spoke of the kindness of America in giving such a fine memorial to the people of the area.

The wording on the memorial is as follows:

THIS MEMORIAL

WAS PRESENTED BY THE UNITED STATES ARMY
AUTHORITIES TO THE PEOPLE OF THE SOUTH HAMS
WHO GENEROUSLY LEFT THEIR HOMES AND THEIR
LANDS TO PROVIDE A BATTLE PRACTICE AREA FOR THE
SUCCESSFUL ASSAULT IN NORMANDY IN JUNE 1944.

THEIR ACTION RESULTED IN THE SAVING OF MANY
HUNDREDS OF LIVES AND CONTRIBUTED IN
NO SMALL MEASURE TO THE SUCCESS OF THE
OPERATION. THE AREA INCLUDED THE VILLAGES OF
BLACKAWTON, CHILLINGTON, EAST ALLINGTON,
SLAPTON, STOKENHAM, STRETE AND TORCROSS,
TOGETHER WITH MANY OUTLYING FARMS AND
HOUSES.

During the ceremony the United States 71st Navy Band, played a selection of musical pieces.

On 10 August 1945, an inquest at Dartmouth returned a finding of 'Death from brain injuries resulting from a fall.' The person in question was Sydney Tom Symons, a smallholder of The Cottage, The Forces, Blackawton. His widow told the inquest that he was not a sickly man, and in all the time she had known him he had never been ill and had not once needed to be seen by a doctor.

Evidence was put before the coroner that after a visit to the local pony races Symons slipped on a path as he was going to feed his calves and struck the back of his head on a chopping block. After his fall he went for a drive in a car belonging to a friend of his and he appeared fine and did not complain of any ailment. He subsequently became ill during the course of the night and was admitted to hospital where he died two days later.

On 7 September 1945, an inquest took place in Plymouth into the death of Mrs Matilda Richardson, who was 70 and lived at Morcomb Farm, East Allington. She died in the Prince of Wales Hospital, Plymouth on 8 August 1945.

The coroner, Mr W.E.J. Major, heard from her son, Mr E.R. Richardson, how he was working on the farm when he smelled smoke in the air. He assumed that his mother had set a fire to burn some rubbish. A short while later he heard her scream and saw her running with her clothes on fire, which consisted of a light summer dress. He ran after her and eventually managed to put out the flames. He then went and telephoned for the doctor.

The coroner asked Mr Richardson what the likelihood was of his mother having used petrol or paraffin to start the fire. Mr Richardson replied that he had found a small tin of paraffin near to where she had lit the fire. The coroner replied that it was more than likely that the paraffin had blazed up and set her dress on fire.

Doctor D.J. Hefferman informed the inquest that Mrs Richardson had died a few minutes after having being admitted to the hospital, with her death being as a result of shock brought on by her extensive burns.

At 3pm on Saturday, 24 July 1954, there was a ceremony at the American War Memorial to mark the tenth anniversary of the D-Day landings. During the ceremony, a startling and never-before-revealed admission was made by the American General Alfred Maximilian Gruenther, who at the time held the position of Supreme Allied Commander, Europe. In 1951, at the age of 52, he was promoted to the rank of Four Star General, the youngest ever in United States history.

> *Seven hundred American soldiers were killed and three landing craft were sunk when, on April 28, 1944, when German E-boats eluded the British Navy's defensive screen and attacked vessels taking part in the training off Slapton Sands for the D-Day landings in Normandy.*

The tragic events which had unfolded on 27/28 April 1944 had been kept a secret. There were those in government and the military who had been well aware of what had happened and had determined to keep the incident a secret. They had even threatened those military personnel who had been involved in the incident with a court martial if they dared speak of what they knew, remembering of course there were some 30,000 men who were involved in the overall exercise, although not in the actual incident itself.

The interesting fact here was General Gruenther's admission that seven hundred American soldiers had been killed. The number of men killed in the incident was more than this. In Ken Small's book *The Forgotten Dead*, first published in 1988, he names 946 men who were killed in Exercise Tiger. It is inconceivable that ten years after the tragedy, the Americans didn't know the number of their own men who had been killed.

Amazingly, US Navy Headquarters claimed that they had no knowledge of the incident, as did the British War Office – two claims that are hard to take seriously. Even Earl Fortescue, the Lord Lieutenant of Devon, claimed to have been unaware of the tragedy at Slapton Sands.

Although it is understandable that the tragedy was kept under wraps at the time, why the American authorities didn't inform the families of the men who were killed after the war was over is unclear.

The morning on the day of the ceremony had been one of drizzle and fog coming in off the sea, although by lunch time the sun was trying its best to brighten up the proceedings as people began gathering at the obelisk near where the Slapton Sands Hotel had stood but which had been destroyed during the occupation of the village in 1944. Although the ceremony saw about 400 people in attendance, a mixture of local residents, holiday makers and officially invited guests, it was the local residents who were least represented.

A detachment of men from the Royal Navy, looking resplendent in their white summer uniforms, with their pristinely polished long bayonets sloped forward, presented arms. Local and county dignitaries were in attendance, along with officers from the Army, Royal Marines and the Navy. When General Gruenther arrived, the general salute was given. After inspecting the Guard of Honour, he was introduced to the assembled dignitaries by Earl Fortescue before standing in front of the new obelisk to give his speech, which was a balance of humour and professionalism. He passed on the thanks of a grateful nation for the facilities provided for their troops who had trained in the village and the surrounding areas.

On D-Day American forces suffered 1,465 men killed, 3,184 wounded, 1,928 reported as missing and 26 captured. Despite the tragedy at Slapton Sands, U Force, who landed at Utah Beach, suffered only 197 casualties, 60 of whom were reported as missing. However, the story was somewhat different for the US 1st and 29th Divisions of O Force, who went ashore at Omaha Beach, as they suffered some 2,000 casualties.

After the unveiling ceremony, selected guests were invited to attend a reception at the Britannia Royal Naval College at Dartmouth given by Captain W.G. Crawford where the guest of honour was General Gruenther.

Chapter Eight

Exercises Fabius, Duck and Fox

Exercise Fabius crossed over with Exercise Tiger and ran between 23 April and 7 May. Its primary function was to provide British and US troops with experience in the tasks that they had been set, so that when the many different facets of Operation Neptune all came together, it had every chance of being a success. Those who were in charge of its planning wanted the exercises to be as close to what the men would have to deal with on the beaches of Normandy as possible. Operation Neptune was the first phase of Operation Overlord, the amphibious landing of troops on the beaches of Normandy.

Fabius consisted of six smaller separate exercises, so as to fine-tune the preparations for D-Day. Not all of them took place at Slapton Sands.

Fabius One involved elements of the 1st Infantry Division, which is a combined arms division of the US Army, and its oldest one, having been in continuous service since 1917. Its official nickname is 'The Big Red One' after its shoulder patch, and it also has the nickname of 'The Fighting Fist'. Also taking part in the exercise were elements of the 29th US Infantry Division, also known as the 'Blue and Gray' because of the colour and design of its shoulder flash. Both units practised amphibious landings on the beaches at Slapton Sands.

Fabius Two – elements of the British 231 Brigade, 50th (Northumbrian) Infantry Division, took part in a large scale amphibious landing exercise at Hayling Island in Hampshire. Before the war the division was part of the Territorial Army, with its main recruiting area falling between the rivers Tyne, Tees and Humber, which is reflected in the design of its insignia. It had been reformed in 1920 and at the time included the 149th, 150th and 151st Infantry Brigades. These in turn included the 4th, 5th, 6th and 7th Battalions, Royal Northumberland Fusiliers, the 4th Battalion, East Yorkshire Regiment, the 4th and 5th Battalions, Green Howards, and the 5th, 6th, and 9th Battalions, Durham Light Infantry.

The 50th Infantry Division was one of only two British divisions to land on the Normandy beaches on D-Day, when it landed on Gold Beach. It had previously seen action in almost all of the major engagements in which

British forces had been engaged in Europe, including the withdrawal from Dunkirk. It had served in North Africa, including the Second Battle of El Alamein, the Mediterranean and the Middle East between 1941 and 1943, making it a formidable and experienced fighting resource.

Fabius Three – elements of the 3rd Canadian Infantry Division practised landings at Bracklesham Bay, which is a coastal bay situated on the west side of the Manhood Peninsula in West Sussex. The remains of a Valentine tank can be found just off the beach in about thirty feet of water. It was of British design and was also made under licence in Canada during the Second World War. During the D-Day Normandy landings the Canadians were allocated to Juno Beach.

The combined Canadian forces sustained 950 casualties on D-Day, most of whom were soldiers from the 3rd Canadian Infantry Division.

Fabius Four – Elements of the British army's 3rd Infantry Division, known at different times as the Iron Division, 3rd (Iron) Division, Monty's Iron Sides or Iron Sides, practised landings at Littlehampton, a seaside resort in the Arun District of West Sussex. The division's logo of three black and one red triangle was designed by Bernard Montgomery. The division had also been earmarked as part of a proposed Commonwealth Corps force to be involved in the planned invasion of Singapore in late 1945 or early 1946. This of course never took place due to the atomic bombs that were dropped on Hiroshima and Nagasaki. But they did go on to serve in the British mandate of Palestine after the end of the war.

Fabius Five and Six were final practices for American and British forces working on how to deal with a build-up of men, vehicles and supplies on Allied beaches during the Normandy landings. If these started to build up on any of the beachheads, this could have had fatal consequences. The need was to move resources forward as quickly and safely as possible to prevent casualties from machine-gun and artillery fire.

If Normandy has gone down in history as the largest amphibious military operation of all time, then exercises Fabius 5 and 6 undoubtedly made up the largest amphibious training exercise of the war. By the time planning for D-Day had reached the stages of Fabius 5 and 6, that was as close to the actual Normandy landings as it was possible to get, which meant that no more significant changes could be made to Operation Neptune at that stage. Operation Neptune was the first phase of Operation Overlord; it was the amphibious landing of troops on the beaches of Normandy.

Fabius 5 was a marshalling exercise for British units who were designated for deployment on Gold, Juno and Sword beaches and included the part of the force that was to leave from the east coast ports and the Thames estuary.

Fabius 6 was also a marshalling exercise for Force B along with British elements who would be leaving from their designated marshalling area as well as ports dotted along the south coast of England, including Southampton. American forces had been allocated specific marshalling areas along with the ports of Weymouth and Portland.

The amount of planning, preparation and attention to detail of the exercises was not only incredible, but it showed how every aspect of the operation had been thought about. They thought about troops hitting the beaches and quickly getting them out of harm's way, they had practised at unloading vehicles and stores onto the beaches, and they had even practised getting into their designated positions in the convoys before crossing the Channel to begin the journey that a year later would lead to the end of the war.

As I mentioned above, the incident which took place over 27 and 28 April 1944 wasn't the only occasion when military exercises had taken place at Slapton Sands. There had been joint US Army and Navy manoeuvres there on 8 January 1944, which were filmed by the US Navy, and which are today available for viewing via the United States National Archives in Washington. The exercise included the debarkation of troops, bulldozers and trucks onto the beach from LCTs.

LCTs were amphibious assault craft specifically used for landing tanks on enemy beachheads. They were initially developed by the Royal Navy and later in the war were widely used by the US Navy. The British had originally called them Tank Landing Craft but later took to using the American favoured nomenclature of Landing Craft Tank.

The manoeuvres included the use and explosion of Bangalore torpedo tubes which were used manually by troops to place under such obstacles as barbed wire to blow them out of the way.

Two days after this, on 10 January 1944, there were a number of American DUKWs and military trucks in Slapton Sands that had also helped to evacuate some of the residents and their furniture from the area. Film footage of this day shows bunk beds being unloaded from the same trucks and placed into one of the houses, as if they were going to be used for military accommodation. The same footage shows Royal Marines, sailors and signalmen, along with US Army officers and military trucks, being loaded and unloaded from a British Landing Craft Mechanised or LCM. The same clip also shows Royal Marines and Royal Navy sailors training members of the US Army at Dartmouth.

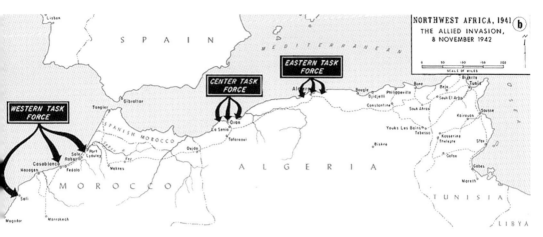

Map showing Operation Torch.

Casablanca Conference, January 1943.

Evacuation at Slapton Sands.

USS *LST – 511*.

LCT 202, English Channel, 1944.

LCTs.

Above: LCMs.

Left: Götz Freiherr von Mirbach.

HMS *Azalea.*

LST *507.*

LCH *98*.

Landings at Slapton Sands.

Sherborne memorial plaque to 294th Engineer Combat Battalion.

USS *Bayfield*.

Left: Lieutenant General Frederick Edgworth Morgan.

Below: General Joseph Lawton Collins, with Field Marshal Sir Bernard Montgomery and Major General Matthew Ridgway.

Earl E Brooks' gravestone.

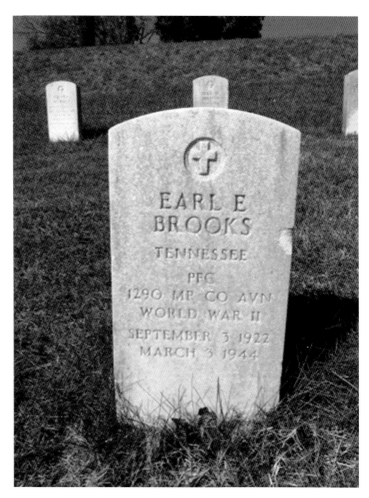

Above left: SHAEF shoulder sleeve insignia.

Above middle: 1st Infantry Division Shoulder Flash.

Above right: 29th Infantry Division Shoulder Flash.

Above left: 50th Infantry Division Insignia.

Above right: Joan Pujol Garcia.

Self-propelled howitzer – 14th Armoured Field Artillery Battalion (*Conseil Regional de Basse-Normandie/National Archives USA*).

Medics on the beach at Normandy.

Elements of 3rd Canadian Infantry Division soon after having landed at Juno Beach.

LST *58* and LST *532*, Normandy 1944.

Exercises at Slapton Sands, April 1944.

Above: American soldiers in Normandy.

Right: General Alfred Maximilian Gruenther.

Above left: General John Waters.

Above right: Joseph Marino.

Slapton Sands Memorial Tank.

Wording on the Slapton Sands
Memorial.

Crerar, Montgomery, Horrocks, Spry and Mathews, Germany, 1945.

THE

TREATY OF PEACE

BETWEEN

THE ALLIED AND ASSOCIATED POWERS

AND

GERMANY,

The Protocol annexed thereto, the Agreement respecting
the military occupation of the territories of the Rhine,

AND THE

TREATY

BETWEEN

FRANCE AND GREAT BRITAIN

RESPECTING

Assistance to France in the event of unprovoked
aggression by Germany.

Signed at Versailles, June 28th, 1919.

[With Maps and Signatures in facsimile.]

LONDON: PRINTED AND PUBLISHED BY HIS MAJESTY'S STATIONERY OFFICE.

To be purchased through any Bookseller or directly from H.M. STATIONERY OFFICE at the
following addresses: IMPERIAL HOUSE, KINGSWAY, LONDON, W.C.2, and 28, ABINGDON STREET,
LONDON, S.W.1; 37, PETER STREET, MANCHESTER; 1, ST. ANDREW'S CRESCENT, CARDIFF;
23, FORTH STREET, EDINBURGH; or from E. PONSONBY, LTD., 116, GRAFTON STREET, DUBLIN.

1919.

Price 21s. Net.

Above: Sir Philip Sasson.

Left: Peace Treaty.

The next film is dated 14 February 1944 and focuses on joint Army and Navy amphibious landings on the beaches at Slapton Sands. Different kinds of naval vessels are used: LCTs, LCIs (Landing Craft Infantry) and LCMs are used during the manoeuvres, and show troops debarking on to the beaches.

In the footage a soldier is seen using a flamethrower, and a number of US Ducks are seen loaded with troops hitting the beaches. Phosphorus smoke shells can be seen bursting on the beach as the troops debark from their landing crafts and an officer is seen standing up in the turret of a tank while he scans the landscape ahead of him through his binoculars. LSTs can be seen on the beach, and on board a tank can be seen with soldiers sitting on its outside as it prepares to embark; trucks and Jeeps ahead of it can be seen leaving the LCT and crossing over barbed wire as they begin to make their way up the beach.

Rockets were fired onto the beach from ships further out in Lyme Bay, while one of the LCTs can be seen firing its 75mm guns forwards on to the beach. Another LCT reverses on to an LST as trucks and Jeeps exit on to the beach from the bow doors of yet another LST.

On 17 March 1944, more amphibious landing training took place at Slapton Sands with LSTs, LCTs, LCIs and LCMs lining up out in Lyme Bay before making their way forward to the beaches where they practised the unloading of men, vehicles and equipment. Also present were two cruisers of the Royal Navy, acting, one would imagine, as escort vessels, the role they undertook on 27 and 28 April 1944.

It appears from the increased intensity seen in the film that they were training for something really big. I wonder how many of those involved realised the significance of what they were doing or what it was leading up to.

There were two other main exercises which led up to Exercise Tiger. The first, Exercise Duck, was held in January 1944. This was, without stating the obvious, extremely important, because any failings or negative observations would determine the direction of Exercises Fabius and Tiger, which were the final dress rehearsals for the Normandy landings.

The decision to activate Exercise Duck had been agreed at a meeting of high-ranking military personnel from the US Army and Navy and the British Army which took place on 21 November 1943. This is interesting as the phone call from the War Office informing the Chairman of Devon County Council Sir John Daw that Slapton Sands and the surrounding area was to become a restricted military area as from 20 December 1943 was received by his office on 4 November 1943 – more than two weeks before the decision to go ahead with Exercise Duck had even been taken.

It was the first major exercise carried out by American troops as they began their training for the D-Day landings. Each unit had to train for their own specific role on D-Day and then carry out further training in conjunction with other units with whom they might have to work alongside.

The first part of the operation was the movement of units from where they were based to their arrival at the assembly areas. There they were processed before being embarked on the correct vessels and in the correct order. Once this aspect of the operation had been mastered, the training then moved on to its next stage, which involved moving the embarked troops from the assembly area along the coastline to the intended beach that they would have to assault. This was the job of the 11th Amphibious Force. Included in this aspect of the exercise was cooperation and communication with the Royal Navy to ensure that the convoy was suitably protected on the journey to its destination from attack by either German submarines or the fast moving and manoeuvring E-boats. The attack convoy was also to be provided with air support by the RAF.

The troops that took part in Exercise Duck were stationed in the areas of Barnstaple, Land's End, Plymouth, and Taunton. Many stayed in tented camps spread out along the scenic and tranquil countryside of the south-west coast of England in such places as East Dartmouth, Falmouth, Helston, Lanivet, Redruth, St Austell, and Truro.

From where they moved to Dartmouth and Falmouth for embarkation to their intended target of the beaches at Slapton Sands.

Some units were also moved to the processing areas in preparation for embarkation only to be immediately returned to their bases to replicate the last-minute cancellation of the operation.

The exercise faced a potential problem in the form of an objection by senior British military authorities who were against the staging of such large-scale exercises along the south coast of England because of the damage that might be done to identified hard-standing areas which were intended for use in the actual invasion operation.

The staff who were required to carry out the logistical work of the exercise, such as arranging the transportation of troops to and from the processing areas, feeding them, making sure the right troops were placed in the right vessels, as well as the security of the marshalling areas, numbered more than 10,000 officers and men. It was a massive undertaking.

The invasion of German-occupied Europe only went ahead after there had been a delay. The same happened on the exercise, although on this occasion it was a delay that had been built in rather than because of inclement weather. The men had already been embarked on 3 January 1944 before the delay was factored in, meaning they had to remain cramped up on board their vessels for an additional twenty-four hours while they waited for the signal to go at 1000 hours the following day. The convoy of vessels, which included a number of LSTs, LCTs, LCIs, LCMs, and LCVPs (Landing Craft Vehicles Personnel), finally left Dartmouth, as had been rescheduled, on 4 January.

There was an extremely interesting fact about this convoy: it was guarded by four destroyers from the Royal Navy, three LCTs that had as part of their armoury 105mm howitzers, and several other fire support craft. Compare this to the tragedy on 28 April in the chilly waters of Lyme Bay when there was just a solitary vessel from the Royal Navy protecting the convoy of nine LSTs that were attacked by E-boats as they prepared to land their cargos onto the beaches.

The landings on this occasion, which were supported by a simulated bombardment of the beaches, went ahead without too much of a problem, although some equipment failed to arrive and some vessels arrived at the wrong time.

For the purpose of the exercise, potential defensive obstacles were assumed, so that the different units who were landing had set objectives, rather than everybody just charging haphazardly onto the beach. A section of the beach had been allocated as having been mined, a nightmare situation for any attacking troops. Imagine heading towards the beach in an open-topped craft, fending off attacks by aircraft from above, while hearing the sound of incoming machine-gun fire rattling against the front and side of the vessel. Then the craft hits the beach, the tailgate comes down and men start getting hit with machine-gun fire and shrapnel from exploding mortar rounds. As if that isn't bad enough, the first man is blown to pieces as he steps on a mine and three of his colleagues are badly injured. This is the reality of what these young men were training for. It was brutal and must have been terrifying.

Other assumed defences included machine-gun emplacements, concrete and steel pillboxes, anti-aircraft batteries, an unknown number of enemy combatants and a variety of armoured vehicles including tanks.

After the beach had been secured and made safe by the infantry units, the support teams made their way in and got to work. Beach exits were put in place and secured. This was an important element of the exercise, because without these everybody was stuck on the beach, which was not a good place to be any longer than was necessary, especially for the initial wave of attacking infantry troops.

Ammunition, fuel and equipment dumps would have been set up. Engineers would have been hard at work laying tracks and improving vehicle ways. Men from the Signals Corps set up loud speaker systems so that troops and vehicle drivers knew where they had to go. Quartermaster and other specialist units were also deployed to test out their equipment, individual tasks and working practices.

The exercise lasted for two days. It had been watched by military observers, and their final report, brutally honest in its content, didn't make for good reading. Security was noted as having been particularly poor.

Out of Exercise Duck I, came Ducks II and III. The assault phase of DUCK II began on 14 February 1944 and lasted for two days. It had already taken two days to get to that stage, with the loading of the vessels completed in the early hours of 13 February. DUCK III took place two weeks later on 29 February, each exercise being an improvement on the last. The following units took part in Exercise Duck:

175th Regimental Landing Team
29th Divisional Headquarters
1st Engineer Special Brigade
IX Air Force Party
Advanced Headquarters V Corps
56th Signal Battalion

Exercise Fox took place over two days on 9 and 10 March 1944 with landings at Slapton Sands. This was intended more as a way of honing the skills needed to master the techniques required for a successful amphibious landing, but it still looked at the marshalling aspect as well. To see what an excellent job the marshalling areas did on this exercise, one only has to look at the figures for military personnel and vehicles that were loaded and embarked from Dartmouth, Plymouth, Portland and Weymouth: 16,923 military personnel and 1,908 vehicles of varying types. There were 21 LSTs, 22 LCT(L)s and 49 LCTs. Along with the other vessels used it would have looked an impressive convoy as it made its way along the coast. As with Exercise Duck, nominated observers watched everything that went on. The units that took part in Exercise FOX were:

16th Regimental Combat Team of the 1st Infantry Division
116th Regimental Combat Team of the 29th Infantry Division
Provisional Engineer Special Brigade Group
37th Engineer Combat Battalion of the 5th Engineer Special Brigade
149th Engineer Combat Battalion of the 6th Engineer Special Brigade
Truck companies
DUKW companies
Medical detachment
Signals detachment
Quartermaster troops
Port troops

Between 4 January and 18 May 1944 there were thirty separate exercises in preparation for the Normandy landings. It is hard to believe with that amount of military activity taking place that Hitler didn't get to hear about it, but as far as we know, he didn't.

Exercise Crackshot took place between 19 and 25 February and was a medical exercise covering the initial treatment by medics on the beach, evacuation to a hospital ship or transportation back to England for the less seriously wounded, and onward transportation to the allocated hospitals which had been set aside for both the exercise and the actual operation.

While researching this book I met a guy who in 2018 was 94 but on 6 June 1944 was a 21-year-old Royal Marines medic on the beaches of Normandy. Sadly for me, but totally understandable, he wouldn't let me interview him about his experiences that day, but what he did say was that it was like 'hell on earth'. It was obvious that even after 73 years he was still haunted by what he saw. Our all too brief conversation was finished by him saying, 'one of the advantages of growing old is that the memories begin to fade and you start to forget things.' Looking in to his eyes, I could tell that there was much that he still remembered.

Exercise Chevrolet began on 25 February and continued until 1 March. It was a marshalling exercise for the 5th Engineer Special Brigade who were amphibious forces of the US Army. This unit had only been formed a matter of months earlier, on 12 November 1943 in Swansea. On D-Day it landed on Omaha Beach. Chevrolet included the training of Chemical Warfare Service troops to hide a harbour and beach by the use of smoke. The location used was Port Talbot. It consisted of:

37th Engineer Combat Battalion
336th Engineer Combat Battalion
348th Engineer Combat Battalion
151st Engineer Combat Battalion – a late addition to the brigade, not arriving in France until January 1945

Exercise Snipe took place over three days, 27, 28, and 29 February, and was an engineering and LST loading exercise at Port Talbot carried out by the 1st Engineer Special Brigade. Although a four-hour time period was allowed for the loading of LSTs, it could be done in as little as two hours. The 1st Engineer Special Brigade was massive and in 1944 had 24 'assigned' units and 65 'attached'.

Exercise Jeep took place between 5 and 31 March and was a marshalling exercise for the 38th Infantry Combat Team which was part of the 2nd United States Infantry Division. An interesting fact about the 38th Infantry is that the first unit to bear that title was the 38th United States Coloured Infantry Regiment, which was founded on 28 July 1866 and served until 25 January 1867. The exercise took place in Northern Ireland where the 38th were stationed. In Belfast docks they went through a somewhat strangely conceived process. The men and their vehicles did not actually embark on any vessels, instead they made their way to the quayside where they waited for thirty minutes to simulate their embarkation. As if this wasn't strange enough, they then walked up a gangplank that had been set up on the quay, before walking down the other side, back on to the quay. That in a nutshell was their training completed. Never having once been anywhere near a ship, they then returned to their accommodation.

Exercise Muskrat I (Beaver I) took place between 12 and 23 March and was for the 12th Regimental Combat Team which was a regimental size fighting unit. They embarked at Plymouth on board three APA-class transport ships before sailing round the coast to the Firth of Clyde where they took part in landing team exercises.

Gull took place between 15 and 18 March 1944 and was an LST loading exercise for the 1st Engineer Special Brigade.

Otter I (Beaver III) also took place between 15 and 18 March 1944 and was an exercise for the 3rd Battalion, 8th Regimental Combat Team.

Mink I (Beaver V) was another exercise that took place between 15 and 18 March, and was for the 1st Battalion, 22nd Regimental Combat Team.

Mink II (Beaver VI) was an exercise which took place at Slapton Sands between 19 and 22 March for the 2nd Battalion, 22nd Regimental Combat Team.

Otter II (Beaver IV) took place between 19 and 22 March and was for the 1st Battalion, Regimental Combat Team.

Muskrat II (Beaver II) took place between 24 and 26 March and was for the troops of the 12th Regimental Combat Team, supported by men from the 1st Engineer Special Brigade. This involved amphibious landings and took place in the Firth of Clyde in Scotland and was a continuation of Muskrat I.

Beaver VII took place between 27 and 30 March for the 8th and 22nd Regimental Combat Teams who were supported by a detachment from the 1st Engineer Special Brigade, along with elements of the 1106th Engineer Group, the 502nd Paratroop Infantry and the 9th Air Force. Those taking part had been embarked at Brixham and Plymouth and sailed around the coast to carry out their assault at Slapton Sands.

Excelsior was a series of exercises, six in total, specifically for artillery sections, which involved units from both the British and American armies. Two of the units that took part were the 29th Infantry Divisional Artillery and the 1st Division's Artillery.

Excelsior I took place on 5 December 1943.
Excelsior II took place on 19 December 1943.
Excelsior III took place between 5 and 9 January 1944.
Excelsior IV took place between 19 and 23 January.
Excelsior V took place 2 and 6 February.
Excelsior VI took place between 16 and 20 February.

These exercises were intended for the benefit of artillery commanders and their junior officers and were held at the British School of Artillery, Larkhill, on the edge of Salisbury Plain.

Crimson II took place between 19 and 20 March and involved artillery, anti-aircraft and tank destroyer units that were part of the V Corps. The premise of the exercise was that they had landed at Slapton Sands and forced the enemy to retreat, attacking them as they pulled back from their initial front line positions. Once they had established themselves on the beach, they then engaged the enemy's new defensive positions.

Spandu was a signals exercise which took place on 4 April with the intention of testing radio communications. It included units from British and Canadian forces.

Jalopy was a replication of Exercise Jeep, just with different units. It also took place at Belfast docks in April 1944, but this time it was the turn of the 10th Infantry Combat Team and the 121st Infantry Regiment.

Splint was a medical exercise which took place on 12 April and focused on casualty evacuation from the beaches. In Normandy it would be for real, under battlefield conditions, with bullets flying about and shells exploding all around. Dealing with wounded soldiers at any time was never easy, but doing so when under attack from all directions and trying to efficiently evacuate them from an active beachhead took a special determination from extraordinarily brave young men. The exercise took place at Pentewan Beach near St Austell in Cornwall. The units that took part in the exercise were:

2nd Naval Beach Battalion
1st Engineer Special Brigade
US Naval Advanced Amphibious Training sub-base

Cellophane took place on 28 April. It was about loading and unloading techniques for cargo from different types of vessels at both ports and beaches. The techniques learnt in this training would eventually be used on the beaches of Normandy, specifically Omaha and Utah. There were other similar exercises which went under the aptly named titles of Cargo and Tonnage.

Pigeon was the second of two communications exercises and took place over four days between 7 and 10 May. It was the final training for the operations that would subsequently take place on Utah Beach.

HAWK was an artillery exercise split in to two parts, the first between 14 and 18 May and the second between 19 and 23 May. Both exercises involved the artillery of the VIll Corps and took place at the Sennybridge Training Area on the outskirts of the Brecon Beacons. The area had been requisitioned as an artillery training area in 1939 and the following year became the location of a Royal Artillery training camp.

Boomerang took place between 19 and 30 April and was a rehearsal for the 9th Air Force. The 5,000 troops taking part in this exercise were observed from three different perspectives: their marshalling process, their embarkation, and finally their setting up of air force dumps on the beaches of an enemy held coastline.

Curveball, with its baseball connections, took place on two separate days. Curveball l took place on 27 April and Curveball ll followed on 6 May. Both days saw the 9th Air Force and the 82nd Airborne Division working together to practise their Normandy invasion tactics.

Eagle was a combined exercise involving the 82nd and 101st Airborne Divisions which took place on 11 May. Both sections were transported by the IX Troop Carrier Command and were dropped under cover of darkness. More troops were landed the following morning by glider. Waiting on the ground were the enemy, played on this occasion by men of the 28th Infantry Division.

Chapter Nine

E-boats

E-Boats (or S-Boots, to give them their correct name) were not covered by the Treaty of Versailles. Their design and construction wasn't restricted by it, possibly because at the time of the treaty's signing in June 1919 such vessels hadn't even been thought of let alone built.

Work on the S-Boot, which was essentially a scaled down warship, began back in 1920, with the ghosts of the First World War still fresh in the memory. They were sleek in design with a robust hull that had to be strong enough to punch their way through the waves of the North Sea. If they could cope there, then the calmer conditions of the English Channel would be a stroll in the park by comparison. They also needed to be fast, very fast.

Different versions were tested through the 1920s before, in 1928, German Naval Command finally decided that a rounded bottom, wooden hull, which reduced weight and so increased speed, would provide the *Kriegsmarine* with what they were looking for.

They turned to the shipbuilder Leurssen, a builder of luxury motor yachts, one of which could travel at 34 knots making her the fastest boat of her class in the world. The contract with Leurssen included additional upgraded engines, for even greater speed, and two torpedo tubes on either side of the bow. So it was that the *Schnellboot* or *S-Boot* or *S-1* came into being.

By the time of the Second World War the S-Boot, or E-boat as it was referred to by the Allies, with the letter E replacing the S to signify the word Enemy, was the workhorse of Germany's *Kriegsmarine*. It became a continuous work in progress, with improvements being made almost as soon as they were reported by the crews. The captain, who in early editions had been stood up in the middle of the structure, entirely open to the elements, ended up in an armour-plated cockpit, which also greatly improved communications on board, saving the captain from having to shout out his orders and instructions at the top of his voice.

By 1943 the armaments on these vessels had been improved, with two 20mm anti-aircraft guns and one 37mm.

The 9th S-Boot Flotilla had had various bases during the war and in the early part of 1944 it moved to Cherbourg to support the 5th Flotilla with operations in the central and western areas of the English Channel, as well as in the North Atlantic, to seek and destroy Allied shipping. The 5th and 9th Flotillas had been extremely proactive and successful in their endeavours. These were very impressive vessels. They were nothing like a pleasure craft. Ninety feet in length and with their powerful Daimler-Benz diesel engines they could reach speeds of thirty-five to forty knots. With their crews of twenty-one men they were able to fire two torpedoes and both 20 and 40mm guns simultaneously.

It is reported that in the late afternoon of 27 April 1944 a German aircraft on a reconnaissance mission in the Channel spotted what it believed was a convoy of Allied merchant vessels in the Lyme Bay region. This information was relayed to the E-boats home base at Cherbourg, and just after 10pm nine vessels from the 5th and 9th Flotillas were deployed.

What the reconnaissance aircraft had actually seen was part of an allied exercise in preparation for the Normandy Landings. The vessels were not, as had first been reported, Allied merchant vessels, they were the Royal Navy's HMS *Azalea* and eight American LSTs. The LSTs were travelling in convoy approximately 700 yards apart at about 4 knots in calm seas for the time of year. Those on the LSTs would have perhaps been a little excited, or perhaps bored, as the training exercises had by that time been continuous for four months. This had usually meant sleeping and waiting on board their LST in a marshalling area, little if any time off, and training exercise after training exercise.

The E-boats crossed the Channel unopposed, somehow managing to pass through a patrol of eight Royal Navy MTBs that had been sent from their base at Portland Bill specially to intercept any E-boats that tried to leave their base at Cherbourg. How did that happen? is the question.

The E-boats then managed to pass unopposed through an outer security line on the mouth of Lyme Bay which stretched between Start Point and Portland Bill consisting of three MTBs, two motor gun boats and four destroyers. Again, these vessels were there specifically to intercept a possible E-boat attack. By 0200 hours the E-boats were in position and ready to launch their attack.

When the soldiers on board the LSTs came under attack, it would have been a massive shock, a total surprise, and a feeling of utter disbelief. Many would have initially thought that whatever was going on was just part of the exercise, added by the planners to keep them on their toes and to see how they reacted. The darkness would have added to the confusion.

The E-boats had an overwhelming advantage, as they knew that they were going into battle and planned accordingly.

The convoy of seven American landing craft should have had two Royal Navy vessels protecting them. HMS *Azalea*, a four-years-old Flower-class corvette, was at the rear of the convoy ready to chase off any unwelcome visitors. At the front of the convoy should have been HMS *Scimitar*, an S-class destroyer which had been launched on 27 February 1918. In the early evening of 27 April 1944, the *Scimitar*, while on its way to Slapton Sands, had been accidentally rammed by LCI number 324 and sustained a large gouge above the water line near her port bow. She returned to Plymouth where she was ordered to remain and have the damage repaired. The captain wasn't entirely happy with the situation, but the decision was out of his hands. An order was an order, and that was the end of the matter. Unfortunately nobody thought to advise the commander of Exercise Tiger, US Navy Admiral Donald Moon.

Commander Geddes, on board the *Azalea*, was aware that the *Scimitar* had left the convoy, but he was unable to inform any of the LSTs. During the original planning of the exercise nobody had foreseen that Royal Navy might need to get in touch with the US Navy, so it was a situation that had never been addressed. They were operating on two different radio frequencies.

The commander of the *Scimitar* assumed that Admiral Leatham, who had ordered him to stay in port and have the damage to his ship repaired, would have organised a replacement. A reasonable assumption in the circumstances, it would be fair to say. But neither the admiral nor any of his staff considered it necessary to do so, meaning that the convoy of seven LSTs had just one vessel protecting them.

Admiral Donald Moon, three months after the debacle at Slapton Sands and two months after the successful landings in Normandy in which he was involved directing the landings on Utah Beach, committed suicide by shooting himself with his navy issue .45 calibre hand gun. The date was 15 August 1944 and Moon's ship, HMS *Bayfield*, was off Naples in readiness for the invasion of southern France which was to begin on that day. It was suggested that his suicide was due to battle fatigue, but perhaps he had not recovered from the events that occurred during exercise Tiger on 27 and 28 April 1944. Having played such a prominent part in the exercise, the loss of so many of his own men must have played heavily on his mind. In moments of reflection, maybe the self-recriminations were too much for him to withstand. He was 50 years of age, married, and left a wife and four children.

The 9th Flotilla consisted of three E-boats: *S-130*, which had been built at the Johan Schlichting boatyard in Travemünde, was under the command of Oberleutnant zur See Gunter Rabe, referred to by his men as The Raven, a nickname acquired because of his nerves of steel and his marauding and carefree style, and a man who led by example; *S-145* and *S-150*. The man in overall charge was Korvettenkapitän Götz Freiherr von Mirbach. The 5th Flotilla consisted of six E-boats: *S-100*, *S-136* under the command of Kapitän Jurgens Meyer, *S-138* whose commander was Oberleutnant zur See Stehwasser, *S-140*, *S-142* and *S-143*. They were under the overall command of Korvettenkapitän Bernd Klug.

With the advantage of surprise, two E-boats, probably *S-136* and *S-138*, focused their attack on just one of the Allied vessels, which turned out to be the last one in the convoy, LST-*507*. Because of its size, and in the darkness, it would have more than likely appeared to have been a merchant vessel. Both of the torpedoes fired by Meyer on *S-136* struck their intended target and one of Stehwasser's also found its mark, which meant the end of LST-*507*. When it went up in flames, it is possible that the German raiders may have believed they had struck an oil tanker.

At about 0230 hours, LST-*507*'s commanding officer Lieutenant Swarts, and his executive officer Lieutenant Murdock, realising the ship could not be saved, took the decision to abandon ship.

The other E-boats quickly joined in the attack, firing their torpedoes at the convoy they had encountered. Some of them, despite firing in the right direction, missed their targets, but what had actually happened was that with the LSTs in effect being flat-bottomed boats, the torpedoes had passed underneath. Maybe this made the E-boat commanders realise that they were not attacking destroyers or cargo vessels.

About fifteen minutes after LST-*507* had been attacked, LST-*531* was the next to fall victim to a torpedo. It suffered its first direct hit at about 0215 hours followed by another a minute or so later. In a short time the LST was on fire and with its power gone was a sitting duck. It would only be a matter of time before the cold waters of Lyme Bay claimed the stricken vessel, so the order to abandon ship was given for the second time that night.

The commanders of the other LSTs now had difficult decisions to make: Did they go to the assistance of *507* and *531* in the hope of picking up survivors knowing that they were putting their own vessels at risk against an unknown enemy, or should they keep well away? They could open fire with their 20 and 40mm guns, but in the confusion would they fire at the right target, and if they fired would they give away their own position?

Independent of each other and in an uncoordinated fashion, *496, 511* and *515* opened fire at actual or perceived targets and LST-*496* inadvertently managed to strafe the deck of the nearby LST-*511* as one of the E-boats sped between them, wounding fourteen members of her crew and four soldiers who were serving with B Company of the 261st Medical Battalion.

One of the crew of LST-*511*, Coxswain E.H. Blazer, received multiple gunshot wounds, mainly down his left side, to his shoulder, chest, hip, both hands, and his left testicle. All of the eighteen wounded officers and men were taken to the Portland Royal Naval Hospital, which was (and still is) situated on the Isle of Portland in Dorset. In 1944 its sole purpose was as a casualty and emergency hospital, which was ideal in the circumstances. Its use as a general hospital ceased in 1940 after it was bombed by German aircraft. During the war Portland had 532 bombs dropped on it in 48 air raids.

LST-*289*, under the command of Lieutenant Harry Mettler, was the last of the Allied vessels to be struck by a torpedo, fired from an unknown E-boat at approximately 0230 hours. Although severely damaged, she managed to stay afloat and eventually made her way back to the safety of Dartmouth harbour. But she did it in a somewhat unusual manner. LST-*289* was carrying, besides other equipment and vehicles, a number of LCVPs, five of which were still in good working order. The decision was made to lower them into the water and place them either side of the damaged *289* so that they could physically lead her back to Dartmouth, which she couldn't do under her own steam due to a broken rudder. During the journey one of the LCVPs broke down and, after her crew were taken off, she was abandoned. Oberleutnant zur See Schirren, commander of E-boat *S-145,* fired one of his torpedoes at it. One can only assume that he did so because he believed it to be some kind of escort vessel, rather than what it was, a landing craft.

The E-boats had sunk two of the LSTs, *507* and *531* and badly damaged another, *289*, as well as having engaged most of the other Allied craft in the convoy. Their opportunist attack had cost the lives of an estimated 749 US Army and Navy personnel. It was just after 0330 when they finally left the area and made their way back to Cherbourg. This was possibly because if they had waited much longer, with dawn approaching, they were in danger of being spotted by one of the many Royal Navy vessels that were now in the area. It was also fortunate for the British and Americans that they left when they did, as if they had stayed much longer they would have had a clearer view of the vessels they had been attacking, as well as sight of the somewhat unusual activity on the beach at Slapton Sands.

None of the E-boats' crew members were killed or wounded during the raid, and all made it safely back to Cherbourg.

On 12 May 1944, two weeks after the mayhem they had caused in the waters off Slapton, *S-130, S-141* and eight other E-boats were on patrol south of the Isle of Wight. They were spotted by the Royal Navy who dispatched a number of destroyers. During the engagement which followed, the French ship *La Combattante* sunk *S-141* with the loss of all eighteen of her crew, one of whom was Oberleutnant zur See Klaus Dönitz, the son of Grand Admiral Dönitz, who for twenty-three days was also the President of the German Reich when he took over the leadership on the death of Adolf Hitler.

The *S-130* also took part in the D-Day landings by attacking the Allied fleet as she made her way to Normandy. She was one of thirty-one E-boats sent from their base at Cherbourg to attack the array of Allied vessels as they approached their allocated beaches. They managed to damage and sink some of the landing craft, but they didn't quite have it all their own way, as two of *S-130*'s crew were killed.

It has to be said that the bravery of the crews of the E-boats was remarkable. They numbered just thirty-one vessels but went up against 4,126 landing craft and transport vessels, as well as 1,213 warships, and also had to contend with being targeted by the Allied aircraft who had gained total supremacy in the skies above the intended landing areas.

S-130 survived the war. For some inexplicable reason her crew decided against scuttling her and she was captured at Rotterdam and taken as a prize by the British who after the war used her for intelligence purposes, even going as far as employing ex-German naval personnel to run her.

The irony for the 110-ton *S-130* is that since November 2004 she has been back in England and is currently being restored to her former glory in Cornwall as part of the Wheatcroft Collection.

Chapter Ten

Those who died on 27 April 1944

There has always been uncertainty about how many men were killed on 27 April 1944; and also what units they were serving with and where they were buried.

Here is a list of American military personnel and the units they were serving with at the time of their death. The list was marked RESTRICTED and was contained in a report dated 30 April 1944. It shows the burial dates of each of those who were buried at the Brookwood American Military Cemetery, which is about 4 miles west of Woking in Surrey.

I am not 100 per cent certain that these are the men who were killed in the friendly fire incident at Slapton Sands on the morning of 27 April 1944, but they certainly fit into the same time frame and, as can be seen from the list below, out of the twenty men buried on 27 April 1944, eleven of them were from seven separate artillery units. The chances of that many men from so many different artillery units dying in unrelated accidents being buried on the same day in the same cemetery is too much to be just a coincidence.

This document was sent to the Quartermaster General's office in Washington, DC:

Those buried on 27 April 1944

William F Carey, 1st Lieutenant O-448328, B Battery, 258th Field Artillery Battalion.

Clifford E Dale, HA 1st Class 762-07-82, LST-436 Medical Detachment, US Navy.

Albert J Fabing, T/5 36724383, 3507th Medium Automotive Maintenance Company.

Lawran R Headley, Private 1st Class 37091782, C Battery, 228th Field Artillery Battalion.

Bronzo L Henson, St. M 2nd Class 587-801, LCI 95, US Coast Guard.

Gordon A Hicks, Sergeant 6970717, A Company, 813th Tank Destruction Company.

William R House, T/5 31100825, B Company, 1st Engineering Company.

Andrew T Hucko, 1st Lieutenant O-1174001, Headquarters, 258th Field Artillery Group.

Thomas A Hughes, Private 34024246, Headquarters Battery, 258th Field Artillery Group.

Edward C Jones, T/5 34332270, A Battery,174th Field Artillery Battalion.

Kenneth S Jordan, Private 1st Class 35250508, 7th Field Artillery Battalion, 1st US Infantry.

William C Krause, Private 1st Class 33130483, Headquarters Company, 2nd Battalion, 56th Armoured Regiment.

Denton Mattis, Private 31332503, 1313th Engineering G S Regiment.

Anthony Pappalardo, Private 34664250, D Battery, 467th Anti-Aircraft Artillery Battalion, Automatic Weapons.

Harry A Ryhal, Tec/5 35131223, 896th Ordnance, Heavy Automotive Maintenance Company.

Raymond S Smith, Private 1st Class 34501322, H Battery, 997th Field Artillery, Battalion.

John P Sousa, Private 31300402, C Battery, 228th Field Artillery Battalion.

Ervin A Stern, Private 1st Class 36122427, C Battery, 228th Field Artillery Battalion.

Harry C Watson, Private 20326758, B Battery, 190th Field Artillery Battalion.

Aaron A Wells, Private 32635995, C Battery, 228th Field Artillery Battalion.

Those buried on 29 April 19144

Walter L Butler, Private (Tec/5) 37137449, 3685th Quartermaster Truck Company.

Armand A Demers, Private First Class 31224834, 2nd Signals Company, 2nd Infantry Division.

Howard G Larsen, 1st Lieutenant O-394744, Headquarters 173rd Field Artillery Group.

Leslie F Oswald, Sergeant 38000204, I Company, 66th Armoured Regiment. This was one of the many units that were involved in the Normandy landings, arriving there on 9 June 1944.

Those buried on 1 May 1944

The following men all served with the 557th Quartermaster Railhead Company, and not, as it said in the document, the 577th. The unit on board LST-*531* when it was attacked and sunk in Lyme Bay had 73 of its officers and men killed and one wounded.

Walter Alexander, Private 32420064.

Chester Barrett, Staff Sergeant 32506520.

William R Battle, Private 36875514.

Floyd E Blake, Tec/4 35410567.

William Blond, Private 3554584.

Jacob A Bohl, Private 36821790.

George E Brown, Tec/5 39396010.

William M Campbell, Private 1st Class 34425815.

James P Cavanagh, Private 32808444.

P D Crawford Jr, Private 1st Class 32085141.

Anastacic De Leon, Private 1st Class 32108629.

Jee Quong Dye, Private 1s Class 32596619.

Herman Eintracht, Private 1st Class 33328846.

William J Follmer, Private 1st Class 35472974.

John P Glass, Tec/5 35416769.

Shirley C Godsey, Tec/5 35444544.

John J Gonshirski, Private 35511468.

John P Hanks, Private 1st Class 34763923.

Ernest P Haynes, Private 32716315.

Alvie M Hogland, Private 1st Class 34390350.

Douglas L Lambert, Private 1st Class 3544446.

Glen R Marcum, Private 20518566.

J A Marino, Private 32220065.

Patty Marino, Private 1st Class 32538043.

Paul H Methner, Private 1st Class 36712742.

James C Mitchell, Staff Sergeant 38119032.

Clarence Monk, Private 1st Class 3440548.

Robert C Morang, Private 1st Class 31217684.

Aloysius G Morgenstern, Private 1st Class 35605272.

Erwin F Morse, Private 1st Class 31206069

Hyman Nathan, Private 1st Class 32821535.

John A Olsen, Private First Class 32860180.

Curtis Pentecost, Private 1st Class 14041607.

Issac W Pritt, Private 1st Class 35444182.

Stephen G Schwartz, Private 1st Class 32337843.

Samuel Silversmith, Private 42035925.

Miles E Sweeney, Private 42030843.

Ernest Tyson, Private 32802841.

John C Veenbaas, Private 37448967.

Mauel Vieira, Private 31137027.
Richard Von Wald, Staff Sergeant 36251672.
Chalcie G West, Private 34438934.
Obie D Willis, Private 1st Class 35605272.
Joseph O Wright, Private 32732324.
Dominick Yanarello, Private 42035605. (In Ken Small's book, this surname is spelt Yangrello, but it is definitely the same man.)
Lawrence C Zempel, Private 1st Class 36266902.

The following three men served with the 1605th Engineering Map Depot Department who were also on board LST-*531* when she was attacked by the E-boats.
George E Hoops, Private 39312785.
Richard E Swanson, T/Sergeant 19016503.
Joseph J Walsh, Tec/3 33099540.

The following men served with the 625th Ordnance, Ammunition Company.
Frank G Harrison Jr, Technician 4th Class 35586178.
Richard L Franks, Private 35595949.

The following men were also on board LST-*531* when she was struck and were serving with the 531st Engineering Shore Regiment.
John J Edwards, Private First Class 35377891.
Clifford F Park, Private 32899794.
Leland Simmons, Private 1st Class 39237054.
George W Steen, Private 32950816.
Harvey J Borchers, Private 1st Class 39308563.
Martial J Bisaillon, Private 1st Class 31053434.
Rocco F Lillo, Private 32926865.
Marshall J Stevens, Private 1st Class 31102109.
William R Elliott, Private 1st Class 35377903.

The following men were also on board LST-*531* when she was struck and were serving with the 33rd Chemical Decontamination Company.
Ralph A Suesse, Captain 0–1035021.
Charles W Sigman, Private 34443424.
Kenneth Clayton, Private 38408572.
John W Strapp, Tec/4 35505209.
Nilo V Bertini, Private 1st Class 33322366.

John Bernardo, Private 1st Class 32409916.
Horace Johnson, Private 34514719.
A J Rosowski, Private 33587420.
Oris A Stokes, Private 31110688.
Harry Mieczkowski, Tec/5 36510674.

The 3206th Quartermaster Service Company was one of the many units that were on board LST-*531* when she was struck by torpedoes fired by the E-boats in Lyme Bay.
Joe V Penalver, Private 18012028.
Lawrence L Muerer, Private 1st Class 37416408.
Paul W Wilson, Private 1st Class 38185187.
Fay E Thomas, Private 1st Class 37504430.
Curtis A Nagel, Private 1st Class 37502727.
Herman D Clark, Private 1st Class 37503147.
Edgar Pope, Technician 4th Class 32554089.
James W Spurling, Private 1st Class 37416680.
Ernest C Bryson, Private 37415508.
William R Reese, Sergeant 1st Class 35003973.
Hoy F Boyles, Private 37503191.
John T Klobe, Corporal 37415642.
Joseph Ciccio, Corporal 37501145.
Metro Butry, Private 33604611.
Dale E Guffin, Corporal 37503381.
Floyd E Wintjen, Private 1st Class 37416334.
Marvin W Groves, Technician 5th Class 37659918.
Alvin G Morgan, Private 1st Class 37504065
Charles R Floyd, Private 37659872.
Dennie Goss, Private 37416264.
Walter Burgfield, Private 37415567.
William L Humphrey, Private 1st Class 37504138.
John H Callahan, Private 1st Class 37416192.
Wallace F Snyder, Captain O-258951.
Christopher T Cope, Private 1st Class 37504179.
John I Mathewson, Captain O-418809.
Salvatore Laiacona, 1st Lieutenant O-357935.
Ezra F Kreiss, Staff Sergeant 33188497.
Otis L Hollon, Private 1st Class 37498733.
William M Kay, Private 1st Class 37415554.

Libro C Cesaro, Private 42002642.
Horace S Williams, Private 38393615.
Blaine L Louder, Private 1st Class 37503238.
Calvin Brecheisen, Technician 5th Class 37503150.
Louis Golfinopulos, Private 1st Class 37415686.
Robert G Chambers, Private 37502173.
Myron A Wright Jr, Private 1st Class 37502117.
Francis L Haile, Private 1st Class 37503825.
Harley E Blevins, Private 1st Class 37504160.
Willard C Sharff, Corporal 37659948.
Melvin A Roberson, Private 37416153.

The following men were also on board LST-*531* when she was struck
   by torpedoes fired from E-boats and were serving with the 607th
   Quartermaster Graves Registration Company.
Clarence C Niedermeier, Sergeant 38377638.
Dominick Caracciolo, Private 1st Class 38377638
Elmer J Saunders, Private 1st Class 35098574.
John C Grevon, Staff Sergeant 39285912.
Luther T Ward, Private 1st Class 34168137.
Nick C Dakis, Private 36666554.
James N Waugh, Seaman 1st Class 827-91-88, was a crewman of the USS
   LST-*531*.

The following four men particularly interest me because they are not
   mentioned as having been on board LSTs *289*, *507*, or *531*. They served
   with the 35th Signal Construction Battalion, and were all buried on 1
   May 1944. Are these possibly some of the men who were killed in the
   friendly fire incident on the morning of 27 April 1944?
Raul J Vannatta, Private 35573665.
Hollis L Nelson, Tec/4 34477215.
Evert M McClatchey, Tec/5 38230181.
Kenneth P Wilson, Tec/5 15324742.

The next three men all served with the 462nd Amphibious Truck Company
   who were one of the units on board LST-*531*.
Simon Van Ess, Tec/5 36463730.
Carl L Schultheis, Private 35756590.
Clarence M Van Nostrand, Technician 5th Class 32858037.

The 3891st Quartermaster Truck Company were not aboard either of the two stricken LSTs, the *507* or the *531*, nor the damaged LST-*289*. Second Lieutenant Harold Kreutz was buried on this day and two other men from this unit were buried on the next.

Elmer J Goodhue, Corporal 31215043.

Christian Misciagno, Technician 5th Class 32682571.

Thomas D Graham Jr, Technician 5th Class 34655706 served with the 3021st Quartermasters Bakery.

The following men served with the 478th Amphibious Truck Company, which was one of the units that were being conveyed by LST-*531*.

Raymond C Joyal, Technician 5th Class 1103104.

Michael A Ogurek, Corporal 32108130.

Ulysses J Catman, Private 325858792.

Edward T Scanlon, Technician 5th Class 36007782.

Herbert A Southcott, Technician 5th Class 32032890.

Paul J Dindino, Technician 5th Class 33311953.

John A Miglionico, Technician 5th Class 32108038.

Charles F Massa, Private 1st Class 6912640.

Harold E Lee, Technician 4th Class 35004178.

John B Brown, Private 34776588.

Albert Mlakar, Staff Sergeant 33032707.

Merle B Humble, Technician 5th Class 33102342.

Roy B Grigsby, Private 34801109.

Herrel K Powell, 1st Lieutenant O-324403.

Sam S Arcuri, Technician 5th Class 32035938.

Those buried on 2 May 1944

Harold E Kreutz, 2nd Lieutenant O-1591251, served with the 3891st Quartermaster Truck Company.

Charles W Hobbs, 2nd Lieutenant O-1315688.

Lester Wright, 2nd Lieutenant O-1641083.

Robert J Conklin, Tec/5 32918383.

The above three men served with the 35th Signal Construction Battalion.

Michael J Di Pasquale, 2nd Lieutenant, 557th Quartermaster, Railhead Company.

Howard R Evans, Staff Sergeant 39459408, Headquarters 6th Company, Armoured Group.

Floyd E Foster, Private 31320307, C Company, 295th Combat Engineering Battalion.

Theodore R Hilliard, Tec/5 39909427, 611th Engineering Light Equipment Company. It is known that up until 21 April 1944 this unit was staying in camp at Perham Downs, Wiltshire, the day before all troops taking part in Exercise Tiger were moved to their marshalling areas.

John W Schneider, Private 36756251, Section 6, Squadron B maintenance Division.

Ray E Seibert, Captain O-1580301, 557th Quartermaster Railhead Company.

William C Teller, Tec/5 32841208, A Company, 299th Combat Engineering Battalion. This unit sailed from New York on board the SS *Exchequer* on 6 April 1944 and arrived in Cardiff ten days later. From there they sailed to Ilfracombe and arrived at the Braunton Hut Camp on 18 April. The unit played an active part and prominent part in the Normandy landings on 6 June 1944.

Clarence H Tomberlin, 1st Lieutenant 557th Quartermaster Railhead Company.

Those buried on 4 May 1944

Raymond F Blizzard, Private 35386552, B Battery, 14th Armoured Field Artillery Battalion. This unit was involved in the D-Day landings in Normandy and the push towards Cherbourg.

Arthur M Dubois, Private 1st Class 36361473, 7th Ordnance Medium Maintenance Company. The men who worked in units such as this one were highly skilled mechanics who could repair or replace the engines of military vehicles or the recoil mechanism on an artillery piece.

John M Flanagan, Private 32859924, A Company, 297th Engineering Combat Battalion.

Marshall R Lockyard, CWO W-2102006, Signal Section, SBS, SOS.

Lawrence E Macdonald, Staff Sergeant 35388045, 3206th Quartermaster Service Company. MacDonald is mentioned in Ken Small's *The Forgotten Dead* as being one of the casualties of Exercise Tiger, and we also know that he was one of those on board LST-*531* when it was attacked and sunk by E-boats on 28 April 1944. The 3206th Quartermaster Service Company had 195 killed in the attack and 9 wounded. This was out of a starting total of 251. Macdonald's inclusion on this document is proof that the men who were killed during Exercise Tiger were buried at Brookwood Cemetery. The only ambiguity is the delay of seven days between his death and his burial. This could have been because his body was not one of those initially discovered, or because it was held in another location, where it was examined before burial. Maybe no such scenario had been considered where such a large number of men would be killed while taking part in an exercise and therefore there was uncertainty as to where any such casualties would be buried.

Those who were buried on 6 May 1944

Joseph Occhipinti, Private 32890847, served with the 557th Quartermaster Railhead Company, which was one of the units on board LST-*531*.

Henry H Hall, Technician 5th Class 35655753.

Lauren M Belshe, Private 17044331. Both of these men served with A Company, 247th Engineering Battalion.

Richard A Borrusch, Private 16064592. Served with L Company, 38th Infantry, 2nd Division.

Those buried on 9 May 1944

Malvin I Weinstein, Private 32976982, A Company, 247th Engineering Combat Battalion (not one of the units involved in the E-boat raids of 28 April 1944).

Lilborn Gates, Private 37499250, 3915th Quartermaster Gas Supply Company.

Robert Flinn, Private 33168171, B Company, 20th Engineering Combat Battalion.

Gilbert Johnson, Private 34713064, E Company, 389th Engineering Gas Supply Regiment.

Silas W Carpenter, Private 1st Class 37228758, F Company, 41st Infantry. The unit had moved to Tidworth Barracks in Salisbury in November 1943 to begin stringent training, which wasn't helped by the poor English weather. In mid-April all passes were cancelled and the men of the 41st were engaged in numerous beach landing operations, some of which, one would imagine, would have been held at Slapton Sands. They arrived on the beaches of Normandy on 9 June 1944 rugged and hardy, all prepared to do their duty. Private Carpenter was certainly in the right place to have been one of those killed in the friendly fire incident of 27 April 1944. We know that his unit were involved in beach landing exercises which, because of where they were staying, would have more than likely meant they were at Slapton Sands; the only obvious question is why it then took eleven days before his body was buried at Brookwood Cemetery.

William J Smith, Private 12024605, served with F Company, 33rd Armoured Regiment of the 3rd Armoured Division.

William Maquire, Private 6148403 of the 87th Armoured Field Artillery Battalion, Headquarters Battery.

Melvin C Kraft, Sergeant 33152663 of the Anti-Tank Company, 175th Infantry Regiment.

Arthur C Early, Private 1st Class 35620556, 408th Quartermaster Service Company.

Kenneth L Wells, Private 39417557, 666th Ordnance Company.

Elvin Battle, Private 35509057, A Company, 459th Signals Construction Battalion.

Without any official confirmation of how many men were killed, and what units they were serving with, it is impossible to be certain that any or all of the men I have mentioned above were casualties of the incident that occurred on 27 April 1944.

Although there are personnel lists available of those men who were killed during Exercise Tiger in the E-boat attack – the Americans only officially confirmed that this incident took place in 1954. But I have not seen a similar admission in relation to the friendly fire incident that took place on 27 April 1944, nor have I ever seen a list of those who died or how many there were.

The weekly report of burials, sheet number 85, which covers the dates 2 to 13 May 1944 and relates to Brookwood and Cambridge cemeteries in England, includes twenty-two names of American servicemen who had been killed and who were buried at Brookwood cemetery during the above time frame. Eleven were buried on either 2 or 3 May 1944. Of these, five were from the crew of LST-*531* and five others were from LST-*289*. A further two were from LST-*280*, although *280* wasn't one of those involved in the raid by the E-boats on 28 April 1944.

There have been different reports of what happened to the bodies of the men who were killed in the friendly fire incident of 27 April 1944, including the claim that they were buried in a farmer's field that was within the curtilage of the restricted military area around Slapton Sands.

The sadness remains that the relatives of these brave young men possibly still don't know how where and why their loved ones died. If that is the case, then it is still wrong and it needs to be rectified by the relevant American authorities.

Chapter Eleven

Those who died on 28 April 1944

There were different ways of doing this but here is how I have decided to record the names of the American military personnel who lost their lives during Exercise Tiger in April 1944.

I have included the names of the men from the army who were on board the two American landing craft that were sunk and the one that was badly damaged off Slapton Sands. I have then broken it down further to the units they were serving with at the time, and those who lost their lives on 28 April 1944. I have then listed the naval men who died from each of the LSTs, separately.

I have started with LST-*507*, the first to be attacked. She was reportedly struck by several torpedoes fired by the E-boats at just after 0200 hours. Only two are known to have exploded, one of which set her on fire. As she began to sink, the E-boat crews allegedly fired on the deck of the stricken vessel, as well as on survivors who had jumped into the water. She was still on fire and had partially sunk some two hours later. At about 0400 a Royal Navy destroyer arrived at LST-*507*'s position to pick up any survivors. The destroyer's captain determined that the nearly submerged vessel, with only her bow now visible above the waterline, should be sunk.

Here are the names of the different units and the men who were serving with them who were killed during Operation Tiger and who were on board LST-*507*:

478th Amphibious Truck Company

John J Allen	Sam S Arcuri	Frederick W Blind
John B Brown	Ulysses J Catman	Robert M Cooke
Samuel J Cut	Bernard Davenport	Paul J B Dindino
Frank Dubisz	Herman Flemming	Roy B Grisby
Harold H Grossman	Merle B Humble	Raymond O Joyal
Harold E Lee	Joseph P Mancuso	Charles F Massa
John A Miglionico	Albert Mlaker	Michael A Ogurek
Herrel K Powell	Clyde C Pritchard	Thomas C Reibel
Edward T Scanlon	Herbert A Southcott	Edward J Unger
Emer O Welch		

557th Quartermaster Railhead Company

Walter M Alexander
Floyd E Blake
Edward L Brown
William M Campbell
Willie J Conner

Michael J DePasquale
Herman Eintracht
John P Glass
John P Hanks
John T Johnson
Douglas L Lambert
Joseph A Marino
Paul A Methner
Clarence Monk

Edwin F Morse
James E Music
Joseph Occhipinti
Leray Pemberton
Victor P Ruoto

Ray E Seibert
Myles E Sweeney
John D Veenbass
Harold Voorhees
Joseph O Wright

Chester Barrett
William Blond
George E Brown
James P Cavanaugh
Arthur L Craig

Troy Dobson
Edwin Fischer
Shirley C Godsey
Ernest P Haynes
Claude E Johnston
Joseph P LoPresto
Patty Marino
James C Mitchell
Robert C Morang

Robert P Motley
Hyman Nathan
John A Olsen
Isaac W Print
Stephen G Schwartz

Samuel Silversmith
James L Tuma Jr
Manuel Vieira Jr
Chalcie G West
Dominick Yangrello

William R Battle
Jacob A Bohl
Terrence V Campbell
Guy Coleman
Poindexter D Crawford

Quong J Dye
William J Follmer
John J Gonshirski
Alvie M Hogland
Elmer L Knight
Glen R Marcum
Wilbur Marts
Norman C Molander
Aloysius G Morgenstern

Raymond J Murphy
Joseph L Noel
Frank Parisi
Lewis Roberts
Conrad J Schwechheimer

Mathew E Strubel
Ernest Tyson
Richard F Von Wald
Obie D Willis
Lawrence C Zemple

33rd Chemical Decontamination Company

John Bernardo
Kenneth Clayton
Harry Mieczkowski
Joseph A Rosiek
Charles W Sigman
John W Strapp

Nilo V Bertini
Clarence O Deakyne Jr
Helmer E Panek
Anthony J Rosowski
George Spitler
Ralph A Suesse

John W Brumfield
Horace Johnson
Quirino A Recchione
James P Sheridan
Horace A Stokes
Stanley K Wood

440th Engineer Company
1605th Engineer Map Depot Detachment

Richard E Swanson   Joseph J Walsh   George Hoops

The 404th did not sustain any casualties during the E-boat attack.

The following men were either members of the US Navy or the US
Naval Reserve and were part of the crew of the LST-*507* whose bodies were
recovered in the immediate aftermath of the incident and were then officially
recorded as killed in action:

James Bailey	Charles D Bennen	John J Bettencourt
Henry A Blackie	James J Clark	James F Cleary
Conner D Collins Jr	James T Crowe Jr	Vincent P Cusack
Carl W Dailey	Thomas J Del Luca, Jr	William W Dickerson
Joseph M Dinneen	Henry R Dobson	James W Durrum
Harold E Eisenbach	Paul R Field	Felton T Fitts
Jake Gambrel	Charles W Garlock	Richard M Gibson
Leonard Goldsmith	Jimmie W Griffen	William T Gulledge
Joseph G Grecco	Raymond R Grehan	Jerry P Hampton
Bruce B Hofman	Russell W Hoffman	Philip E King
Louis F Karasinski	Theodore J Koski	Alvin L Ledbetter
Howard A Martin	Daniel W Maggard Jr	Joseph M Moore
Edgar F Morancy	Robert C Mackey	John H Miller
Lester A Meyers	John E Matthews	Robert J Malott
Michael J O'Connell	James P Ryan Jr	Charles G Raptis
Paul M Ragusa	William L Rogers	Henry Q Saucier
William H Schreiber	Kennan H Smith	Lawrence P Squiers
John L Stanesic	Charles J Staudt Jr	George A Sullivan
Pete J Sutherland	J S Swarts	Deward W Woods
Curtis M Wright		

The following, from the crew of LST-*507*, were initially reported missing
in action but were later confirmed as having died on 28 April 1944, either
by their bodies having been found or because they were never found. Those
who were initially classified as missing in action had their status changed to
killed in action on 8 July 1944.

Sylvester M Burns	Francis A Carroll	Nelson Grunther
Frank T Lighty	Malcolm F Sturdivant	Andrew Watson

Frank L Whipping   Harold M Weinbrot   Richard E Ricketts
Robert E Saxon   Kenneth L Scott   Steve J Trgovic
Joseph E Tully

The following is a list of the men from the US Army who were killed at
Slapton Sands on 28 April 1944 when LST-*531* was sunk by E-Boats:

3206th Quartermaster Service Company

Ovid C Adcock   Alvin E Aid   Delmar R Allen
Joe M Arismendiz   Marion J Asberry   Raymond Baldwin
Calvin C Banister   Ralph E Barber   Ralph A Basgall
James R Baugus   Walter B Bergfield   Howard G Bird
Louis L Birkley Jr   Thomas J Blethroad   Hartley E Blevins
Bernard E Bonderer   Wilfred G Bost   Hoy F Boyles
Portter J Bratton   Calvin D Brecheisen   Ivan J Brown
Ernest C Bryson   George W Bruckner   Robert E Burke
Floyd H Burks   Harold Burns   Robert T Burrell
Metro Butry   Jay H Cain   Paul J Caldwell
John H Callahan   Ernest Carey   George P Cates
Libro C Cesaro   Richard L Chamberlain   Robert G Chambers
Donald H Childs   Arthur F Chudzinski   Joseph Ciccio
Ott S Circle   Herman D Clark   Francis M Coan
Woodson D Constant   Christopher T Cope   James O Cottrell
Harold E Crandell   Carrell S Crane   Thomas C Creed Jr
Edd W Crocker   Homer L Dame   Fred S Danner
Thomas Daoukas   Franklin W Davis   Morris J Debaene
Paul R Dehass Jr   Joseph F DeSalvo   Garland D Donaldson
Earl V Douglas   John M Douglas Jr   Meredith J Duckworth
Johnnie O Duncan   William A Duncan   Ralph T Earnest
Roy E Eckhoff   Mathews J Edleman   Bill E Edwards
Carl M Elliot   Nicholas J Evangelist   Junior T Farris
Darrell D Ferguson   David E Fizer   Arthur A Fletewall
Charles R Floyd   Adrian L Ford   Joseph H Frank Jr
Hershel G Freed   Leslie W Friend   Joseph A Galuppi
John L Gasser   Donald E Gephart   Hilmer L Gieschen
Bill E Gillespie   John W Glasscock   Melvin R Glaze
Louis J Golfinopoulos   Dennie Goss   James P Gray
Marvin W Groves   Dale E Guffin   Francis L Haile
Ern F Harrington   Peter J Heffernan   Lester Hobbs

Otis L Hollon
Francis L C Hudson
Clifford E Hutchinson
George A Kielbasa
Johnny D Kladus
Ezra F Kreiss
Champ D Libla
Blaine L Louder
Patrick J Mahoney
Robert E Manes
Louis B McCampbell
Harry W Mattler
Alvin G Morgan
Robert T New
Delbert E Overton
Marvin L Payton
Jon V Penalver
Charles E Picking
Charles J Pshenitzky
Walter W Reitzal
Alvin E Richardson
Ralph R Roberts
Harold L Sanford
George R Sitche
Wallace F Snyder
James W Stephenson
Louis A Tenuta
Mearl L Toerber
Jacon Trager
William A Turk
Everett E Whitelock
Vernon S Wilson
Frederick J Wolpert
Mike J Yadrick

Robert L Hopkins
William L Humphrey
William M Kay
William E King
John T Klobe
Walter V Larson
Evan W Long
Earl C Lowrie
John Mallassi
Ralph D Marsh
Roy E McKinnon
Laurence L Meurer
Hugh C Murray
Aubrey L Newman
Johnnie D Owens
Cleo B Peake
Milton Penn
Alfred E Poggi
Thomas E Raines
Lowell L Renner
James E Roberson
Rudolph J Roper
Willard C Sharff
Steve L Smerek
William F Sparks
Lennie C Sutt
Joseph A Tesoriero
John N Tolie
Stanley H Treef
Howard W Wagner
Horace S Williams
Floyd E Wintjen
Darryl Wooderson
John W Yates

Albert H Hovis
Arnold Hurt
Otto W Keller
Bertram Kinkead
William Korodi
Clarence E Lasswell
Joseph D Long
Lawrence E MacDonald
John V Manak
Haskel H Mayfield
William F Meehan
James E Miller
Curtis A Nagle
Lawrence W Ott
James E Park
Luther M Pearson
Lindsay Peters Jr
Edgar F Pope
William R Reese
Irving Rettinger
Melvin A Roberson
Raymond G Salemmo
John P Sheahan Jr
Wallace W Smith
James W Spurling
Owen A Tate
Fay E Thomas
Victor M Torres
Luther R Tucker
Gerald A Watson
Paul W Wilson
Russel L Wirt
Myron A Wright Jr

531st Engineering Shore Regiment

Martial J Bisaillon
Donald S Bryant

Harvey J Borchers
John J Edwards

Wayne R Brewer
William R Elliott

Lester J Gardner
Rocco F Lillo
Gerrit Peters
Marshall L Stevens
Grady D Webb Jr

Everett W Jordan
Theodore G Lowell
Leland Simmons
Joseph H Tousignant

John A Kapinos
Clifford F Park
George W Steen
Hillard Tuttle

607th Quartermaster Graves Registration Regiment

Alexander R Marvin
Edward J Delamater
Robert E Holmes
Elmer D Stillwell
Larry R Wier

Louis A Bolton
John C Grevon
Thomas B McCormick
Ernest M Thompson
Dominick Caracciolo

Nick G Dakis
Ravila Herbert
Clarence C Neidermeir
Luther T Ward
Elemer J Saunders

462nd Amphibious Truck Company

Albert F Alsip
Allesantro Cutrone
Lawrence R Flynt
Eugene Gamer
Eugine A Henley
Richard H Jensen
John H Levengood
Frank F Mattos
Trinidad Mercado
Joseph L Ostrowski
Harry Ruediger
Joseph H Sessamen
Marvin L Summerall
Henry F Wolfgram

John J Clardy
Stephen J Czyzniak
Russell Fontana
William A Garrison
Charles W Hobbs
James G Johnson
Samuel S Loper
Earl M McMore
Michael J Naccarelli
Ulton A Ray
Richard C Schleyer
Michael J Shatkawski
Imon Van Ess
John E Wyckoff

Robert J Conklin
Oscar L Drawdy Jr
Salvadore D Ford
William Gray
Stephen J Holzberer Jr
Robert B Leishman
Wilbert V Lyon
Robert H Megathlin
Ubron M Ogden
Robert R Riggs
Carl L Schultheis
Donald E Snider
Clarence M van Nostrand

HQ's 1st Engineering Specialist Brigade

Salvatore Lalaconia

John I Mathewson

625th Ordnance Ammunition Company

Carl M Bean
Richard L Franks

John A Delitko
Herbert S Garvin

Alexander G Donaldson
Walter Gearhart

Frank G Harrison Jr	Louis S Patou	Tracey V Rohrbaugh
Jesse E Smith	Glen T Strader	Denver Walker

It appears from the records that nobody from either 4144th Quartermaster Service Company or the 35th Signal Construction Battalion were killed during Operation Tiger.

The following were either serving with the US Navy or the US Naval Reserve and were part of the crew of LST-*531* who died as a result of the incident at Slapton Sands on 28 April 1944:

Allen O Achey Jr	Norris G Brock	Ellis W Baugher
Elmer C Benton	Floyd H Bolling	Vincent M Callas
Frederick C Carr	Eugene R Cowan	Michael J Coyle
Glen H Dawson	Harold C Denton	Richard W Edson
J J Gallaher	Charles Harrell	John H Hill
Samuel D Holmes	Bernard A Hauber	Eugene Hayth
James W Hurley	Walter P Jackman	Edmond L Jacques
Mark F Kessinger	Ralph Kirkwood Alexandra	Harold D Kuhns
Alexander Krizanosky	Ford H Kelley	Charles G Land
Hollace H Leeman	Burvil E Lacey	Harry Levine
L H Levy	Melvin L Locklear	Tiffany V Manning
Ralph R Miller	Doyle D Montgomery	Cornelius J Parker
Williams Pear	James D Peters	William J Petcavage
Daniel R Schumanske	Edward A Sochaki	Thanuel V Sheppard
William Solomon	Steve J Stemats	Lyle F Showers
Alvin C Unger	Albert J Vandeland	Lloyd L Witten
James M Waugh		

The following were also members of the crew of LST-*531* who were either from the US Navy or the US Naval Reserve. They were originally listed as missing in action but their official status was changed to killed in action on 8 July 1944:

Williard C Anderson	J W M Behrens	Arthur H Bliss
Wade L Bridgham	Clifton H Brummitt	W H Cantell
Ralph O'C Cason	William W Cobern	Richard L Colwell
Richard V Corideo	A F Cram	Curtis W Croswell
Joseph Cruz Jr	Eugene F Cummings	William J Czerwinski
Harry I Danley	Edward G Debias	Theodore D Degouff
Edwin J Dobson	Robert G Drake	Ralph O'C Duffy

K C Fisher
Samuel Goldstein
Robert J Hartman
Albert J Jencovic
Albert P Kaska
Emery E Marcus Jr
William J Merrill
Robert D Peterson
John E Poloncarz
John M Shea
Edward Stoklosa
James W Walls
Ernest T White
Raymond J Christoffel
Joseph L Starr

Hobart Ford Jr
Murray B Gurn
Lawrence E Hopkins
Albert W Johnson Jr
Reuben G Kerby
Frank A McGuen
Kermit H Neil
Kenneth Phillips
Daniel L Ruguai
George Shengarn
George W Taylor
Robert G Walters
Ray Borgerson
John J Ellis
L O Nelson

Edward A Gaboys
William C Hall
Melvin J Jansen
Henry Kartz
Grady E Kirby
Robert W McLean
Elisha G Noble
Richard Pogue
Gail E Samuelson
Walter A Spangler
Willie W Townsend
Raleigh F Watsch
William E Brickey
James O Scott

There were no known army personnel aboard LST-*289* who lost their lives on 28 April 1943.

The following were either serving with the US Navy or the US Naval Reserve and were part of the crew of LST-*289* who died as result of the incident at Slapton Sands on 28 April 1944:

Mitchel L Broske
Mike G Hackes
Herman R Kortenhorn
Clifford L Roberts

James W Chandler
James H Harvie
Robert M May
John L Shipp Jr

Joseph W Griffin
Earl V Muza
Harold A Neff

The following two men were initially reported missing in action but, as with those from the other LSTs, their official status was officially changed on 8 July 1944 to killed in action:

Walter H Farzier   William C Muller

The list below is of other individuals killed during Operation Tiger but which I have been unable to establish the LSTs they were on board at the time:

818th Port Battalion

Leroy Daniels   Harold G Foster

556th Quartermaster Railhead Company

Arastacio Deleon   Michael Mance

While researching this aspect of the book I viewed the website longshoresoldiers.com where I saw a post by a Mr Gerard Marino in relation to his father Joseph Marino. I was slightly confused by the post as in it Gerard wrote that his father had served with the 531st Engineer Shore Regiment. The confusion was on my part because I had seen that Private Joseph A. Marino had served with the 557th Quartermaster Railhead Company and had been one of those lost when LST-*531* was sunk. My immediate assumption was that this was Gerard Marino's father, but, remarkably, it wasn't.

Gerard Marino's father was Joseph Marino, but he was a private first class who served with the 531st Engineer Shore Regiment. In the early hours of 28 April 1944, men of the 531st Engineer Shore Regiment were on board LST-*507* when it was attacked and sunk by E-boats. One of those men was Joseph Marino. By the time the attack was over, nineteen of Joseph's friends and colleagues were either dead or missing. On 1 April 2018, I received an e-mail from Gerard. Here is some of what he had to say:

> Well, the facts are my father did not serve with the 557th Quartermaster Railhead Company, and he did not lose his life with LST-531 in Operation Tiger. My father, Private First Class Joseph Marino, served with "C" Company, 1st Battalion, 531st Engineer Shore Regiment, 1st Engineer Special Brigade.
>
> On D–Day the 531st Engineer Shore Regiment was assigned to the 4th Infantry Division, when they assaulted Utah Beach, Green Sector.
>
> I have read a book about the 531st Engineer Shore Regiment, which is entitled "Storming Ashore" by Kenneth Gam, and it recounts the missions of the 531st from North Africa, Sicily, Salerno, Normandy and Holland.
>
> Amongst the back pages of the book were the casualty lists from Operation Tiger, which were laid out per each of the units that took part, and there to my amazement I saw listed Joseph A Marino, buried Brookwood Cemetery, England (B, F-1-79). However, the book lists on page 238, a Joseph A Marino who was on board LST-507. This is probably the man you believe is my father, but it isn't.
>
> My father joined the 531st Engineer Shore Regiment in England after his training at Fort Belvoir, Virginia. He told me that the men from his new Unit, had only recently arrived from fighting in Salerno.

The Americans carried out amphibious landings at Salerno on 9 September 1943. The 531st Engineer Shore Group would have been part of the 5th Army Group under the command of General Mark Clark. For some reason the decision had been taken to carry out the landings without carrying out either any Naval or aerial bombardments. Even more bizarre, as American forces made their way to the beaches at Paestum, they were met with the sound of a voice from a loudspeaker, in English, coming from the landing area they were heading to: 'Come on in and give up. We have you covered.' The request was ignored and the fighting began. It continued until 17 September, by which time some 190,000 Allied soldiers had been landed on the Italian mainland, of which more than 12,000 became casualties: 2,000 killed, 7,050 wounded and 3,500 missing.

> *From then onwards, he was involved in training for the Normandy landings, although they didn't know at the time what they were specifically training for, but it wasn't hard to guess. My father took part in Exercise Tiger, and I can recall him telling me of the horrific happenings that occurred during the Exercise.*
>
> *After they had recovered from the rigours of what had happened during the Exercise, and just six weeks later, they set off for Normandy, which he again survived. From there the 531st Engineer Shore Regiment, went on to St Mere Eglise, Cherbourg, Carentan, St Lo, then on through Belgium, Holland and Germany. I recall my father telling me he was in Maastricht in Holland and Aachen Germany. During his time near Aachen, my father met up with his brother, my Uncle, whom was with "E" Company, 311th Regiment, 78th Infantry Division, who had just survived a horrific battle at Kesternich, Germany.*

Gerard's reference to Kesternich relates to one of two sets of possible dates, as there were two battles of Kesternich, which took place in quick succession. The first was between 13 and 16 December 1944, and the second from 30 January to 1 February 1945. I believe his reference to his uncle being part of the 311th Regiment was actually the 311th Regimental Combat Troop, as they are shown as having taken part in both battles.

Both Joseph Marino and his brother survived the war and made it back home to their friends and family in America.

Chapter Twelve

The BIGOTs – Who were they?

There has been much discussion about the BIGOTs since the tragedy at Slapton Sands in April 1944.

What did BIGOT refer to? It was a reference to the level of security that a man could be given in relation to Operation Overlord; it meant above top secret. Anybody with a BIGOT security clearance possessed vital information about a particular aspect of the invasion of Normandy, but not necessarily the entire picture from top to bottom. With there being so many different aspects to the invasion, a man only needed to know what was going to be relevant to him, what he and his men would be doing and the beach they would be landing on during the D–Day landings. An engineering unit wouldn't need to know what an infantry unit had been tasked with, and airborne units wouldn't need to know what targets a warship had been given. It is not totally inconceivable that many of those in possession of a BIGOT security clearance did not know the specific destination to which they were headed. But each part of the jigsaw helped build the overall picture.

The name BIGOT had its origins in the 1942 Allied invasion of North Africa. The documents for that operation might be marked 'To Gib' – a shortening of Gibraltar. This has then been spelt in reverse to form BIGOT. How this was then subsequently arrived at as a security level I have absolutely no idea, other than to guess that a member of the planning team possibly had a little too much time on his hands.

In the immediate aftermath of the E-boat attack, there was concern, trepidation, and even panic when it was discovered that ten of those with BIGOT level security clearance were missing.

As dawn broke on 28 April 1944, there were hundreds of bodies floating in the sea drifting inland towards the beaches at Slapton Sands. Navy divers were sent in to retrieve the dog tags from the bodies. The matter of immediate importance wasn't to identify all those who had perished, but rather to search for the names of ten particular individuals who had BIGOT status security clearance. There is no record that I know of that has survived the passage of time which names those ten individuals. All I can do is have an educated guess at who they might have been.

Captain John Mathewson served with the HQ's 1st Engineer Special Brigade, which by the time of Exercise Tiger was already an experienced unit. They had first arrived in England in August 1942 and in December took part in the North African campaign. They went on to take part in the Allied invasion of Sicily, then the invasion of Italy in September 1943, and returned to England before Christmas to commence their pre-Normandy invasion training.

Captain Ray E. Seibert was one of the seventy-three men serving with the 557th Quartermaster Railhead Company who were killed when LST-*531* was sunk by one of the E-boats in Lyme Bay during Exercise Tiger.

Most of the American servicemen who died in the early hours of 28 April 1944 had been on board LST-*531* when it was struck by a torpedo and set on fire. There were 142 Navy personnel on board the *531* of whom 114 died. One of those who survived, and the ships only officer to do so, was Ensign Douglas Harlander, who dived into the water as the ship's hull dropped beneath the waves.

There were also 354 Army personnel on board of whom 310 were killed. Captain Wallace Snyder was a member of the 3206th Quartermaster Service Company, another of the units being transported to Slapton Sands on board LST-*531*. When the casualty figures were finalised, or as best as they could be in the circumstances, Snyder's unit had lost 195 of its officers and men.

Captain Ralph A. Suesse served with the 33rd Quartermaster Decontamination Company, Chemical Warfare Service, during Exercise Tiger. He was a holder of the Purple Heart, a decoration awarded to personnel who are wounded in action. Suesse was a married man who had enlisted on 7 March 1941. It is interesting to note that when his parents and his wife were informed of his death by the Adjutant General's office in Washington, all they were told was that he had been killed on 28 April in the European theatre of war. That was it. Nothing else. There was no information concerning how or where he died.

Out of the known lists of the servicemen who perished as a result of the E-boat attack in Lyme Bay, there are only five who held the rank of captain, a rank one could expect to have been entrusted with information about the impending landings at Normandy. Having exhausted the list of captains who were killed in Lyme Bay, I looked at other ranks to see if I could come up with a total of ten men. This is what I found:

Lieutenant Edward J Delamater, 607th Quartermaster, Graves Registration Company.

Lieutenant Salvatore Lalacona, Headquarters 1st Engineering Special Brigade.

Lieutenant Herrel K Powell, 478th Amphibious Truck Company.

Lieutenant Clarence H Tomberlin, 557th Quartermaster, Railhead Company.

Lieutenant James L Tuma, 557th Quartermaster Railhead Company.

I now had five captains and five lieutenants, from different army units, ten in total, who took part in Exercise Tiger and who were either killed or missing. Whether they were the BIGOTS referred to in the story of Exercise Tiger, I have no way of knowing for sure, but it seems inconceivable to me that men from other ranks, no matter how good they were at their job, would be entrusted with such vital information ahead of a ranking officer.

There were also twelve officers from the US Navy or the US Naval Reserve who were crew members of the three torpedoed LSTs, *507*, *531* and *289*, who were killed in the E-boat attack and could have been BIGOTS as well. These were:

Lieutenant J S Swartz.
Lieutenant Kennan H Smith.
Lieutenant Bruce B Hoffman.
Ensign James J Clark.
Ensign Conner D Collins.

All the above were part of the crew of LST-*507*, although it is unlikely that either of the ensigns, Clark or Collins, would have been BIGOTs. All five were members of the US Naval Reserve.

The following were crew of LST-*531* serving with the US Royal Naval Reserve, while Lieutenant Behrens was a member of the US Navy:

Lieutenant L H Levy.
Lieutenant John H Hill.
Lieutenant Tiffany V Manning.
Lieutenant J W M Behrens.
Ensign Walter P Jackman.
Ensign J J Gallaher.

Ensign A F Cram.
Ensign L O Nelson.
Ensign W H Cantrell.

On the topic of BIGOTs, in 1983 Gunther Rabe, who had been in command of E-boat S-*130* during the raid on the American LSTs on 28 April 1944, wrote, 'My boat fired two torpedoes at about 0205 am. As there were many ships in the area, we could not attempt to close in to look for survivors.' Assuming that this was also the attitude of the other E-boat commanders on that fateful night, and the fact the Rabe never made any mention of his colleagues having picked up any survivors, it is fair to suggest that collectively they not only had no idea of the importance of what they had stumbled across, but had no suspicions about the ships they had attacked being anything other than a merchant convoy, travelling under the cover of darkness, and close to the coastline for their own safety.

During the Second World War, Heinrich Müller was the permanent chief of the *Reichssicherheitshauptamt Amt IV*, more commonly known as the Gestapo. He was involved in the planning and execution of the Holocaust, and remains the most senior figure of the Nazi Party to have neither been captured nor confirmed dead. The last known date Müller was confirmed alive was 1 May 1945 in the *Führerbunker* in Berlin.

In 1980, private correspondence and files purported to have belonged to Müller turned up in Switzerland. These ended up being forwarded to CIA Headquarters at Langley in the USA. Part of this treasure trove included an 800-page, postwar interview between Müller and an unnamed American intelligence officer conducted in Switzerland. If this is true, then Müller did not die in the *Führerbunker* on 1 May 1945. It would appear that at the time of the interview he was still a free man, which is relevant as if he had been under arrest at the time there is perhaps more likely to have been an attempt at falsification.

Part of what he told his interrogators related to Exercise Tiger. He claimed that an agent of theirs had alerted them to a large Allied exercise that was taking place at Slapton Sands, and that after the subsequent raid, off Lyme Bay, one of the E-boats had returned to its base with a copy of documents that had been recovered from a dead American officer mentioning the intention for the invasion of German-occupied Europe to take place at Normandy. He further said that this information was passed up the chain of command, but was dismissed as a bluff, as it was still believed that any such attack would take place at Calais.

This of course contradicts in part what Gunther Rabe stated in his 1983 letter, and is highly improbable. Firstly, the E-boats were involved in a fast moving raid where their survival was dependent on their ability to move quickly between the vessels they were attacking, so how would they have had the time to slow down and search through hundreds of bodies to find an officer. Secondly, although there were BIGOT officers on board the stricken American LSTs, any knowledge they would have had concerning the impending invasion in Normandy would have been in their heads and not contained in bundles of papers they would have been carrying.

Chapter Thirteen

Aftermath of Exercise Tiger

Because of the tragedy at Slapton Sands on 28 April 1944, US General Joseph 'Lightning Joe' Lawton Collins, commander of VII Corps, wanted an assessment carried out to determine what had gone wrong and what lessons could be learnt to ensure that the same mistakes were not made on the beaches of Normandy.

Collins was a vastly experienced military man whose service went back to the First World War. He was one of only a few senior American commanders to have served in both the Pacific and European theatres, and he went on to become Chief of Staff of the US Army during the Korean War.

His older brother, James, was a major general who also served in both the First and Second World Wars and whose sons were Brigadier General James Lawton Collins and Major General Michael Collins, US Air Force Reserve, the latter being the same Michael Collins who in July 1969 was part of the Apollo II crew that saw man step onto the moon for the first time.

The assessment wasn't going to be easy. Depending on what he found, Collins might have to make negative comments about some of his fellow, senior officers. He mentions the delay in H-Hour on 27 April but, interestingly, he makes no mention of a friendly fire incident on that day. That can only be for two reasons: either because no such incident took place, or because it did take place and he was involved in ordering that no mention of it be made.

Collins mentioned the confusion that the H-Hour delay caused for his troops, but didn't expand on that point any further. How did it cause confusion? – that's the question that needs answering.

Moving on to the 28th of April: Nine LSTs laden with equipment and 30,000 troops had left various marshalling points on the south-west coast on the evening of 26 April to simulate the time it would take to cross the English Channel before arriving at Slapton Sands. The LSTs were escorted by two destroyers, three torpedo boats and four gun boats. On the following day, there was only one escorting vessel, an aged corvette, HMS *Azalea*. Ultimately, this decision was the responsibility of the Royal Navy who were part of the southern command under Admiral R. Leatham.

How could one convoy have had nine naval vessels escorting it while the next, which took the exact same route and was going to be doing the same exercise, was allowed to set off with only one escorting vessel? Was it a breakdown in communications, an error of judgement, an incorrect assumption, or very poor leadership by inexperienced officers. Surely the man in charge had a check list to go through before allowing the exercise to begin? The whole point of training exercises was to iron out mistakes. That clearly didn't happen when it came to Exercise Tiger, which was the culmination of some thirty other exercises. Tiger was the final dress rehearsal for Operation Overlord and the D-Day landings.

It is reported that American soldiers who were playing the part of German defenders on the sea front at Slapton Sands were given live ammunition to fire at their comrades. It has even been suggested that in Exercise Tiger they fired into their own men. This supposedly resulted in the deaths of American soldiers, with rumours being in the hundreds rather than just a few. I find this very hard to believe. Neither the American military, nor political leaders past or present, have ever made any admissions of this incident having taken place. If it did, and resulted in hundreds of deaths, there are no known records.

One of the lessons learnt from Exercise Tiger was a very simple one: life belts. It was determined that many had died because they had worn their life belts incorrectly. Instead of wearing them up under their arms as was intended, many had worn them lower down and even around their waists. As soon as they entered the water their life belts pushed them forwards from the waist down and, with the weight of their sodden kit as an added burden, they fell face down, were unable to right themselves, and perished. Addressing this one simple aspect of the tragedy and ensuring that every single man was fully instructed is believed to have saved many lives during the course of the D-Day landings. Having said all of that, it is absolutely staggering that the issue of men wearing their life belts incorrectly only came to light in the final dress rehearsal for D-Day, and then only because hundreds of troops were drowned.

A somewhat strange decision concerned the use of DUKWs, or rather their non-use. DUKWs had proved useful during Operation Husky, the Allied invasion of Italy which began on 9 July 1943 and included American forces. The landings took place across a 105-mile stretch of beaches and 160,000 men, 600 tanks, 14,000 other vehicles and 1,800 artillery pieces came ashore. This was a year before the Normandy landings and, intentionally or otherwise, was a dress rehearsal for that operation.

Operation Husky wasn't perfect by any stretch of the imagination, but it was an overall success. One of the successes was the use of DUKWs to take supplies from the LSTs and other vessels to the beach. DUKWs could also be used for transport inland once a beachhead had been secured, whereas the use of an LCT basically came to an end once it reached the shoreline and the tailgate dropped onto the beach. Despite this, Admiral Moon, who was in command of Exercise Tiger, didn't want to use DUKWs but the less effective LCTs instead.

Communications had proved to be a flaw. Firstly, it was recognised that British and American radios were set on different frequencies and therefore couldn't have spoken to one another even if they had wanted to. Secondly, when the LSTs had been struck by the German torpedoes, the communications on the vessels had been put out of action which prevented officers from giving instructions over the loudhailers: men were left having to guess whether or not they should jump overboard, which led to panic. It transpired that there were signs on each of the LSTs which addressed this very issue, but nobody had bothered to point these signs out to the men on board.

A problem with Exercise Tiger, and other exercises for Operation Overlord, was that they just did not appear to be taken seriously enough by some American forces. Apathy was the order of the day. All too often, officers and men alike went through the motions, doing just what they had to and no more. Men knew that they would embark onto a nominated vessel, leave their marshalling area, sail around the coast, arrive off Slapton Sands, disembark onto the beach, run across the sands, take out pretend enemy positions, wait to be told that the exercise was over and then go back to their home station.

Maybe because of the shock of what happened at Slapton Sands, the realisation suddenly dawned on all taking part that they were up against a real enemy and lessons were learnt. One way or another, the training which took place between January and May 1944 in and around Slapton Sands and in the South Hams region of Devon, helped save the lives of many young Americans.

Chapter Fourteen

A soldier's memories

While researching for this book I came across eight letters. They don't reveal any new, never-before-heard-of information, and because of military restrictions they reveal few facts, but they contain the thoughts of a man who is preparing and training for war.

Private 35235353 Charles R. Young of B Company, 304th Engineer Combat Battalion of the 79th US Infantry Division arrived in England via the port of Liverpool on 17 April 1944. From there he travelled by train to Devon where he took part in amphibious training exercises before landing on Utah beach on D-Day plus six: 12 June 1944. Young and his colleagues waited a week before seeing their first action: it was on 19 June when their war began in earnest with an attack on the high ground just south of Cherbourg. Young then spent the next year fighting his way across Europe, via France, Belgium, Czechoslovakia, and Germany before finally, 248 days later, arriving in Hammelburg in Bad Kissingen, Bavaria.

During the Second World War the town was the site of two German prisoner of war camps. There was the Oflag Xlll-B camp, which was for officers, and was part of a large German Army training camp, which had been in the town since 1873. Its initial use during the Second World War, was for Yugoslavian officers, who had been captured during the Balkans campaign, which took place between 28 October 1940 and 1 June 1940.

American officers who had been captured at the Battle of the Bulge arrived at the camp on 11 January 1945. Two months later on 10 March, and after an eight-week, 400 mile forced march from the Oflag 64 camp in Szubin, Poland, more American officers who had been captured earlier in the war during the North Africa campaign, and the Battle of Normandy. This brought the total number of American's in the camp to 1,291 officers and 127 enlisted men. An International Red Cross visit and inspection of the camp on 25 March 1945, reported that conditions there were very poor.

Oflag Xlll-B was the scene of a liberation attempt on 27 March 1945, which had been ordered by General George S Patton. What was called Task

Force Baum, which was some 300 strong, and included a total of 57 vehicles, arrived at the camp to liberate the American prisoners who were being held there, only to find they had bitten off more than they could chew. However, intelligence reports about Hammelburg proved to be inaccurate, and the mission turned in to a failure. The Americans had 32 of their men killed, about 230 were captured and taken prisoner, with only 35 managing to make it the 50 miles back to Allied territory.

The question has always been asked why did the operation go ahead in the first place, especially as the end of the war was just a matter of weeks away. Why put American lives at risk so close to the end of the war. It might be prudent to point out at this stage, that one of the American officers who was being held at Oflag Xlll-B, was US Army General John K Waters, who had been captured and taken as a prisoner of war, while fighting in Tunisia, North Africa in 1943. He was also the son-in-law of General George S. Patton, and married to Patton's daughter, Beatrice.

Ironically, one of the American soldiers wounded during the attempted liberation, was, General Waters, when he was shot by one of the camp guards, although badly wounded, he survived, and continued serving in the Army until 1966.

The second camp, Stalag Xlll-C, was for enlisted men and non-commissioned officers. Those held there included American soldiers captured at Normandy and the Battle of the Bulge. Captured Allied soldiers from Yugoslavia, Belgium, Holland and France, were also held there.

The first of the letters Charles Young sent was to his brother Paul back home in America, dated 3 May 1944. The envelope shows an address of 301 Wadsworth Avenue, Meadsville, Philadelphia, USA. Paul was also a private (339265170), although the unit he was serving with had been crossed out. The letter didn't arrive until 19 June 1944, some six weeks after it had been sent, and five days after Charles had landed in Normandy:

Dear Bro,

Sorry to hear that you are laid up for the present time. Got a letter from Betty and she says everybody is getting along fine. Well Paul, this finds me somewhere in England. I made the trip ok, was a little sick the first day, but soon got alright. It is quite different here from what we are all used to. The custom of living is a lot different. Well Paul, I do not know much news so cannot write much.

You take care of yourself and write me the news. I have not heard from dad yet. If you get a chance, try and buy me a small cigarette lighter, sure could use one.

Your Bro.

The letter had been sent by what was called V-Mail (Victory Mail), which was a hybrid mail system employed by the United States throughout the Second World War. It was the primary means by which American servicemen stationed overseas on active service could securely correspond with their families back home. Letters were read through by the military censor, copied to film, and then printed back to paper on arrival at their destination. A large number of letters could be reduced to a thumbnail size image on microfilm, and tons of shipping space could be saved, allowing it to be used instead for war materials. For example, 150,000 one-page letters would require 37 mailbags to transport them, whereas the same number of letters on microfilm only required one mailbag; 45 lbs in weight down from 2,575.

The second letter was dated 9 May 1944 and was sent while Charles was training in England. This time he wrote to Miss Betty Young, at the same address as the one he wrote to his brother Paul. I assume she was his sister:

Dear Betty,

Hope this finds you all well and that Paul is getting along ok. I am ok, and got a letter from Ola, and she says she has gone back to work, so I guess she is ok by now. I got a letter from Dad and he is not working yet. It was wrote April 3rd, so he should be working now. I do not think he will find it as easily as he did back east.

Well, Betty you may send me a box of Candy, and a lot of other stuff. Well, Betty, it's the same old story, not much news and tell everybody "Hello" and to write.

Love
Reno.

I am guessing Charles's middle initial stands for Reno, as that's the name he signs the letter with. It is interesting that he says 'not much news'; the reality probably was that he had plenty of news and wanted to talk about it, but because of war time restrictions he was unable to do so. At the time of writing Charles would have been training for three weeks.

Ten days later he was writing again, again to Betty, this time with the kids included, at the same address:

Dear Betty & Kids,

Just a few lines to let you know I am still in Great Britain.

Hope this finds you and the kids ok. It has been several days since I have heard from any of you, I got a letter from Ola last night and she says she is much better now and at work.

I guess you have your lovely garden planted by now. I wrote Paul a letter and have not got any answer yet. Have only heard from Dad once since I saw him in Chicago, I guess he is doing alright. Well Betty, I do not know any news so will not write much.

You tell everybody "Hello" and to write, and let me know how Paul is getting along.

> *Lots of Love*
> *Reno.*

So the censor allowed Charles to mention he was still in Great Britain. I noticed a tone to this letter which was almost one of desperation. His need to hear from members of his family back home was almost palpable. In relation to not receiving a reply from his brother Paul, having written a letter to him, one which he had only posted on 3 May, he obviously hadn't grasped that it wouldn't arrive until 19 June, by which time Charles would have already arrived in Normandy.

The next correspondence has a postmark of 23 May 1944 stamped on the envelope but the letter is dated 17 May:

Dear Betty & Family,

Received your letter today and glad to hear from you and that everybody is well. Sure glad Paul got back home and is feeling better. I sure would like to be back in time when that garden is ready to pick. But time will tell. Got a letter from Yola and Ola today, they are all ok, and getting along. Ola is talking of going back home to stay a while this summer.

Well folks, I do not know of any news to write so will cut this short, and tell everybody "Hello" and to write.

I will try and do better next time. You may send me a box of home made candy.

> *Love*
> *Reno.*

This shows how important the sending and receiving of letters was during a time of war, for young men separated from their family, possibly for the first time, miles away from home, training completed and waiting around before going off to war, not knowing if they were going to be killed or survive.

The next letter I have is dated 28 June 1944, two weeks after he had landed in Normandy and nine days after the 79th Infantry Division had first been in action. I don't know if there are any other letters missing from the sequence:

Hello Paul & Family,

Hope this finds you ok and back to work. I am ok, got lots of mail today. Heard from nearly everybody.

Well Paul, I do not know much news yet, will write a longer letter in a few days. Tell everyone to write, and not to worry about anything. I got a letter from Dad and he says he is ok and making good. I wonder if mother ever went to see him. I guess not.

Will close and hope to hear from you all soon. Say "Hello" to everyone.

Love
Reno.

This letter really got me wondering whether I had misinterpreted the date of the other letters. This letter is dated 28 June 1944, which is some sixteen days after Charles landed on the beaches of Normandy, yet in the letter he makes no mention whatsoever of either being there or even having left England. By now the invasion of German-occupied Europe was three weeks old and had been widely reported in the press, so it was far from being a secret on 28 June.

Had the letter by Charles been written and sent before he had left England? That would explain the total lack of any mention of where Charles was or what he was doing.

His next letter is dated 29 July 1944. As with his previous efforts, this one is short, but for the first time he talks about the military matters he is involved in:

Dear Paul & Betty,

This finds me ok and located in a hayfield. If you follow the papers real close, you can tell about where I am. On the Normandy Front. We sure got Jerry on the run and sure hope this all soon comes to an end.

I got a letter from Ola and she is in Texas having some time, but will go back to Chicago about the first of August. How do you like the work by now? I guess Stanley is still there, they do not want much.

I have to write Dad and then I will be caught up. Tell everybody "Hello" and to write and tell me the news.

Love
Reno.

Finally, Charles's family knew where he was, and while he was most probably overjoyed at finally being able to tell them where he was and what he was doing, they were most probably worried about him.

The next letter was dated 3 September 1944:

Dear Paul, Betty and family,

Received your letter a few days ago and I will scribble a few lines, this finds everything ok, and hope we will soon be on the road home, although I do not hear much news. I have not heard from anyone for several days. I guess you are all busy.

Ola stayed only two weeks at Dallas and she is back at work. Mola and Jack will probably go back to Alabama by winter. So Ola don't know if she will stay at Chicago or not. Well, I must close as space is short.

Love
Reno.

Logistically, it must have been difficult for the mail to follow the troops, especially as their location could change at short notice at any time. Between 15 June 1942 and 1 April 1945 over half a million pieces of (V) mail were sent to American troops serving overseas while a similar number were sent by them to their friends and family back home. A lot of mail was also sent by conventional means, which for many still remained the preferred option, possibly because it allowed more to be written down. It was noted by the Smithsonian National Postal Museum that in 1944 US Navy personnel who were deployed overseas in different theatres of war received 38 million V-mail letters, while in the same time period received 272 million pieces of normal first class mail.

The last letter I have is dated 7 January 1945:

Dear Bro,

Received two letters from you yesterday, dated November 20th and December 4th, always glad to hear from you. I hope you soon get on your feet again. Glad to hear Dad is ok and getting along. Not much news to write about. In answer to your letter. I have been in all of them and sure makes a fellow feel old. The highest number will hit it for the present. You write and I will tell you if you guess right, and on the right, for the time being.

If all the people would wake up and do something this might come to an end and do something about it. Instead of making plans of what they are going to do with the soldiers and the people over here after the war, before it is won.

Well Paul, space is short and I am tired to, [sic] time to rest my eyes.

Tell everybody "Hello" and to write. Tell old lady Schuas to write, anybody at all.

Love
Reno.

I wonder if Paul has been sick or injured and is back home recuperating? It is clear that Paul has asked Charles questions about where he is, what he is doing, casualties, that type of thing, thus Charles says, 'you write and I will tell you if you guess right.' It is also clear that he wants the war to be over with.

After six days of heavy fighting, elements of the 79th Infantry Division took Fort du Roule, finally entering Cherbourg on 25 June. For the following seven days they held a defensive line before moving off southwards to their next destination of La Haye du Puits. The men of the 79th were involved in fierce house to house fighting as the Germans doggedly defended the town. Victory was finally gained on 8 July.

Lessay was the next target which was reached and attacked on 26 July after crossing the River Ay. The advance continued southwards passing through Avranches and Pontorson. From there they turned south–east and headed towards Fougères and Laval, after which they crossed the River Sarthe before entering Le Mans on 8 August. There they only encountered light resistance. Then they moved north to Le Merle sur Sarthe before continuing their advance through the French towns of Longny, Nogent-le-Roi and Mantes-Gassicourt.

Having reached the Seine by 19 August, the 79th established a bridgehead on the river's east bank, where thankfully they met little in the way of German resistance. The division's commander, General Ira T. Wyche, received a telephone call at 2135 hours that evening from General Haislip, commander of XV Corps, who ordered him to get his men across the Seine that night. This is where Charles and the 304th Engineer Combat Battalion came into their own: a bridge was needed across the Seine strong enough to take tanks. But on the evening of 19 August the area was experiencing a downpour of torrential rain. If the 79th Division were going to get their men across to the west bank of the Seine as ordered, it was clear that it wasn't going to be crossing a bridge. Instead a nearby dam provided a narrow footpath for men of the 313th Infantry to walk across in single file.

At first light on 20 August the 304th Engineer Combat Battalion were able to take soldiers of the 314th Infantry across the river in engineer assault craft before returning and commencing the building of the bridge. They did a remarkable job and it was completed the same afternoon, allowing men of the 315th Infantry to drive across in their trucks. By dusk the bulk of the division, including tanks and artillery, had also made it across.

The Germans tried their best to destroy the bridge and the Americans brought up the 23rd Anti-Aircraft Artillery Group to defend it from air attack. Over the next two days they shot down a remarkable forty-three German aircraft and the bridge stayed intact.

The 79th Division continued on to Meru and Mouy while having to fight their way through heavy German counter-attacks between 22 and 27 August. They then crossed the River Therain on 31 August. There was to be no respite as they continued on through Tricot and Rosières on their way to the Belgian border near St Amand. From here they were transferred to the XV Corps and then started heading south, passing through Valenciennes, Cambrai, Soissons, Reims, Vertus, Lesmont, Joinville, and Neufchâteau.

When they reached Charmes on 12 September they encountered heavy German resistance, which resulted in close quarter street fighting, and the town suffered much damage, as it had also done during the First World War.

The 79th crossed over the rivers Moselle and Meurthe before further action clearing the Forêt de Parroy between 28 September and 9 October. They followed that up with a further engagement against German defensive positions to the east of Emberménil between 14 and 23 September.

On reaching Lunéville they had time to rest and, somewhat surprisingly, they even did a bit of training. The tranquillity of their time at Lunéville was broken when they crossed the rivers Vezouze and the Moder on 13 November and became involved in more fighting.

Between 18 November and 10 December at Haguenau they came up against stiff German resistance and experienced some furious fighting at Gambesheim. While in defensive positions they beat off repeated German attacks at Hatten and Rittershoffen during an eleven-day battle, after which they withdrew and took up defensive positions south of Haguenau along the Moder on 19 January, where they remained until 6 February. For the rest of the month and into March they took part in what would be some of the last mopping-up operations of German pockets of resistance.

Charles Young survived all of this, and after the war was over, returned to his home in New York.

Chapter Fifteen

The Missing Men

An interesting article appeared in the *Western Morning News* on 15 April 1998, which also appears on the website of exercisetiger.org.uk. The article concerned a US Army captain, Ralph Green:

Evidence is mounting that hundreds of soldiers were killed by their own side in a tragic training accident on a west county beach in the run up to D-Day. Officially, all deaths in Exercise Tiger have been attributed to enemy action against the tail end of a convoy code named T-4 at sea on the morning of April 28, 1944. Now the WMN has uncovered corroborating testimonies, many breaking a vow of silence for the first time, which suggest hundreds of men were killed in a "friendly fire" massacre 24 hours earlier, soon after the exercise began. During April 1944, former American Army Capt. Ralph Greene was stationed at Kings Wear when suddenly on the 27th he was drafted to help with "several hundred" bodies being transported to Sherbourne Hospital in Dorset. He remembered being briefed by a Colonel that they were expecting soldiers' bodies, some with injuries and hypothermia. "I went to ask what had happened. He said no questions were being taken," said Mr Greene, who now lives in Chicago, Illinois.

This obviously relates to the friendly fire incident that occurred on the beaches at Slapton Sands on the morning of 27 April 1944, of that there is no question, but what is unclear is what subsequently happened to their bodies, and what were their next of kin told about how, when and where they died and where their remains were buried. I would expect that their families received a telegram informing them of their deaths. I would also assume that they were informed where their loved ones were buried.

There are, as I see it, two questions that need answering. Firstly: why has the lie and the subsequent cover-up about their deaths continued for so long? It is understandable that because of the imminence of D-Day and so as not to negatively affect the morale of American soldiers that it might have been covered up for a time. But once the war was over and there was no longer any need for secrecy, why not come clean?

Secondly, who ordered the cover-up? Was it a military decision or a political one? Did Eisenhower make the decision, or was it President Roosevelt?

There are also suggestions that there were other losses of American military personnel on at least two other occasions during the early months of 1944, which I have already commented on in a previous chapter. If friendly fire incidents had taken place during the exercises Duck, Fox and Tiger, why have they never been disclosed? The opportunity certainly arose with the sudden death of Roosevelt on 12 April 1945: Eisenhower and the incoming president, Harry S. Truman, could have wound it up and laid the blame on Roosevelt. But they didn't. Why not? Possibly because the incidents never happened; but if they did then the question remains.

If the friendly fire incidents did take place, then the decision to cover them up could have only come from the very top of the chain of command. That means either Eisenhower, Roosevelt, or possibly both. It is almost inconceivable that one would have known about these events without the other.

Ok, let's look at both men. Roosevelt first. Born on 30 January 1892 to a wealthy New York family, on 4 March 1933 he became the 32nd President of the United States. A Democrat who won four presidential elections, he is seen by many as one of America's greatest ever presidents. His cousin Theodore was president of the United States for eight years from 1901-9. The last of Roosevelt's terms of office began in 1944, by which time his health was already seriously declining. He would have remained in the White House until 1948, but he died in office on 12 April 1945 at the age of 63.

How much he would have been damaged by the scandal over a cover-up of the deaths of American soldiers in England can only be guessed at, but even if he had survived, his failing health would have more than likely prevented him from seeking re-election for a fifth term in 1948.

Eisenhower stayed in the army after the war, initially becoming military governor of the US occupation zone in Germany. In November 1945 he returned to the USA and became Chief of Staff of the Army. There had been moves afoot to get him to run for the presidency as early as 1943. Despite a number of prominent individuals, including Truman, encouraging Eisenhower to run for president in 1948, he declined, saying that he was 'not available for, and could not accept nomination to high political office. Lifelong professional soldiers, in the absence of some obvious and overriding reason, should abstain from seeking high political office' (quoted in *Eisenhower, the President* by Merio J. Pusey,1956).

Despite this, in June 1952 he resigned his NATO command and began campaigning full time for the Republican Party's nomination. Still retaining his enormous wartime popularity, on 4 November 1952 he became president.

If the stories and subsequent cover-up of friendly fire incidents and the disposal of the bodies of American soldiers without a proper burial had come to light at the time, it would have undoubtedly damaged Eisenhower's reputation and popularity and possibly ruined his chances of becoming the nation's President in 1952.

I have to reiterate what I said earlier, there is no official record of the deaths of large numbers of American soldiers during the period January to May 1944 who were allegedly killed during friendly fire incidents, other than the 217 names I have listed below.

The following information has been gleaned from the weekly report sheets that list the deaths of American military personnel who were serving in the European theatre, and specifically in England. The dates of these reports cover the period 1 January to 31 May 1944 and should therefore include every soldier who died during that time while stationed in England. The dead were sent to the Quartermaster General's office in New York. Most were buried at Brookwood Cemetery on the following dates. I have also included men who were buried at the Cambridge American Cemetery during the same time period.

I have not included air crews, or anybody who was serving in the navy unless they were directly connected to an LST at the time of their death. The first two entries are dated December 1943, but only because this coincides with when Slapton Sands and the surrounding area were evacuated by and handed over to the American Military authorities:

23 December 1943

Sergeant 38090828 Jimmie L Richardson, C Company, 827th Engineering Battalion.

24 December 1943

Private 1st Class 36231314 Willie R Cripps, 1978th Quartermaster Truck Company.

4 January 1944

Private 38127402 C R Tidwell, I Company, 531st Engineer Shore Regiment.

Private 1st Class 11019542 Aladar Szentmiklosi, E Company, 26th Infantry Regiment, 1st Infantry Division.

Private 39566954 Kenneth L Fulmer, 333rd Engineers.

Private 1st Class 34363647 Coy H Dunaway, 333rd Engineers.

Technician 3rd Class 35280178 Paul W Taylor, C Battery, 376th AAA.

2nd Lieutenant O-1037296 Robert E Shaver, Army Transport Security Service.

6 January 1944.

Warrant Officer W-2105518 Frank A Traures, 188th Signals Rep Company.

Technician 4th Class 15012103 Leonard W Harter, Anti-Tank Company, 39th Infantry.

8 January 1944

Corporal 12025877 John R Miller, H Company, 18th Infantry.

11 January 1944

Technician 5th Class 21580630 Henry B Donnelly, 1956th Ordnance Depot Company.

Staff Sergeant 32549151 James R Akins, 626th Quartermaster Repairing Company.

Technician 5th Class 34042393 Cordell W Litchford, 869th Ordnance Company.

Private 1st Class 37071523 Harn Kock, Headquarters Company, 3rd Battalion, 36th Armoured Division.

Private 38300008 Coy L Herrington, B Company, 390th Engineers.

13 January 1944

Private 20610292 Leroy L Duskiewicz, A Company, 254th Engineers Combat Battalion.

Private 1st Class 36225849 Russell P Priniski, A Company, 254th Engineers Combat Battalion.

Private 1st Class 20635581 Edward Ripstra, A Company, 254th Engineers Combat Battalion.

Private 39908121 Mark E Anderson, A Company, 254th Engineers Combat Battalion.

Private 1st Class 39263414 Harry L Schechter, Headquarters Company, 3rd Battalion, 121st Infantry.

Staff Sergeant 34145549 Charles F Bradburn, 14th Replacement Control Depot.

Technician 4th Class 6398350 Shular T Freeman, C Company, 813th Tank Destroyer Battalion.

15 January 1944

Sergeant 13022863 Homer C Sarver, 3rd Battalion, 506th Parachute Infantry Regiment.

Private 1st Class 30407249 Juan M Cruz, 245th Quartermaster, Service Battalion.

18 January 1944

Mr Charles K Adams (Civilian) 47th Company, American Field Service (During the Second World War, American men aged 17 to 55 who were deemed physically unfit for military service, but who still wanted to do their bit, could volunteer to join the American Field Service. They were paid $20 a month, became ambulance drivers and stretcher bearers, and were, in the main, attached to British Army Units).

Technician 5th Class 32970838 Carlo Varonn, 2037th Engineers Battalion.

20 January 1944

Captain O-408659 Burt H Strasburg, 634th Tank Destroyer Combat Regiment.

25 January 1944

Private 1st Class 35387652 Henry L Trent, 1192nd Military Police Company (was buried at Cambridge American Military Cemetery).

27 January 1944

Technician 5th Class 31206376 Antone Semas, C Company, 37th Engineer Combat Battalion.

Private 39554185 John F Harris, 16th Replacement Control Depot.

Private 32214240 John Dumhlis, B Company, 45th Armoured Medium Battalion, 3rd Division.

Private 1st Class James R Skidmore, D Company 707th Military Police Battalion.

Private 39605390 Sherwood W Blasdel, 505th Parachute Infantry Regiment, 82nd Airborne Division.

29 January 1944

Corporal 37166348 Emil R Yanish, 8th Mobile Reclamation and Repair Unit (was buried at Cambridge American Military Cemetery).

1st Lieutenant O-886191 Robert M Grove, 1666th Conversion Unit, 12th Replacement Control Depot.

1 February 1944

Sergeant 35511779 Theodore F Lee, 3512th Quartermaster Truck Company.

Private 31315202 Samuel Hamad, B Battery, 129th AAA, Automatic Weapons Battalion.

Sergeant 35500448 Pete J Monty, 326th Airborne Engineers Battalion.

Private 1st Class 32329590 Jacob Mutterperl, Headquarters Company, Trains, 2nd Armoured Division.

Private 37288266 Fred W Chapman, 197th Quartermaster Gas Supply Company.

5 February 1944

Private 37518646 Jamie L H Jones, 308th Quartermaster Railhead Company (was buried at the Cambridge American Military Cemetery).

Private 32097032 Adam E Magoa, D Company, 506th Parachute Infantry.

Private 33047991 Adam P Couch, F Company, 16th Infantry.

Corporal 38285499 John M Gallman, 48th B.A.D., Supply Division Section.

8 February 1944

Private 34458191 Barnie J McQueen, B Company, 392nd Engineering Regiment.

Private 1st Class 33368286 Wilson E Strauser, 4th Reconnaissance Troop.

Technician 5th Class John B Potter, 13th Replacement Control Depot.

Corporal 16065254 Eldridge Billups, C Company, 392nd Engineers.

Staff Sergeant 20317880 Jesse W Cubbler, A Company, 103rd Engineering Combat Battalion.

2nd Lieutenant O-1113679 Donald E Ellson, A Company, 103rd Engineering Combat Battalion.

Sergeant 33022850 Joseph W Kushlick, A Company, 103rd Engineering Combat Battalion.

Private 12127728 William E Nesbitt, 461st Signals Construction Battalion.

10 February 1944

Private 35552105 Marvin J Thornton, A Company, 830th Engineering Battalion.

Private 32337934 John H Waters, 2912th Disciplinary Training Center.

Corporal 33534917 Roger Wilson, B Company, 544th Quartermaster Battalion.

Private 1st Class 3570178 Carl E McCombs, 3205th Quartermaster Company.

Captain O-358146 John W Butcher, Headquarters & Headquarters Detachment, 569th Quartermasters Battalion, 10th Replacement Depot (was buried at the Cambridge American Military Cemetery).

Sergeant 31115683 Wendell F Pratt, 746th Tank Battalion (was buried at the Cambridge American Military Cemetery).

12 February 1944

Technician 5th Class 33640929 Clyde G Morton, 1310th Engineer Regiment (was buried at the Cambridge American Cemetery).

Private 36665235 Lawrence H Sanders, C Company, 707th Military Police Battalion.

Temporary Sergeant 32500770 Joseph Bachmann, 77th Quartermaster Battalion, APO 511.

Technician 5th Class 353070034 Leonard B Robinson, C Company, 374th Engineering Regiment.

Private 32921169 Phillip E Jackson, C Company, 374th Engineering Regiment.

14 February 1944

Technician 5th Class 32285810 John J Mitchell, A Company, 803rd Tank Destroyer Battalion

15 February 1944

Private 33640882 William T Brooks, D Company, 1310th Engineers.

Private 1st Class 33728666 Clinton E Hite, C Company, 374th Engineers Battalion.

Private 36390789 Alonzo Wilder, C Company, 374th Engineers Battalion.

Private 1st Class 20364723 Charles R Jackson, F Company, 116th Infantry, 29th Division.

Midshipman 1st Class 707-69-73 Charles J Cardigan, Headquarters Company Landing Craft.

Sergeant 38056788 James P Rowe, C Company, 23rd A.E. Battalion, 3rd Armoured Division.

17 February 1944

Private 38392026 Mack Littin, B Company, 374th Engineering Regiment.

Private 37502730 Thomas Baggerly, A Company, 37th Engineers Battalion.

F 1st Class 625-39-58 James R Bradley, USS-LST-357.

Private 18105987 Cornelius C Cox, A Battery, 440th AAA Battalion.

Private 20625912 Jack A Buerstetea, Headquarters 6816th Replacement Battalion.

19 February 1944

Private 33827588 George R Dilzer, B Company, 195th AAA Battalion.

Staff Sergeant 32073449 William S Duncan, A Company, 51st Armoured, Infantry Battalion, 4th Armoured Division.

Private 34703368 Julies D Gardner, H & S 207th Engineer Battalion.

Corporal 32320805 Nicholas Guiliane, E Company, 531st Engineer Shore Regiment.

22 February 1944

Technician 5th Class 37449761 Joe V Navratil, B Battery, 457th AAA Battalion (was buried at the Cambridge American Cemetery).

Private 1st Class 32202212 Archie A Bianco, Headquarters, 3rd Battalion, 32nd Armoured Regiment, 3rd Armoured Division.

Staff Sergeant 33024093 Nathan Sonnenfeld, 112th Infantry.

Private 1st Class 33217968 Paul E Thomas, 729th Railway Operating Battalion. (This is interesting, because in February 1944 the unit was based in Manchester undergoing 'extensive military training' and were housed in a large exhibition building at the Bellvue Racecourse. It is unclear why an American soldier who died in Manchester would be brought all the way to Surrey to be buried.)

24 February 1944

Corporal 34467385 Wallace S Rodwell, C Battery, 225th AAA Battalion.

Private 33072346 Joseph F Masterson, B Company, 17th Armoured Engineer Battalion.

1st Lieutenant O-1635193, Johnny A Parrigan, 303rd Signals Company (was buried at the Cambridge American Cemetery).

29 February 1944

Captain O-333080 Roderick F MacDougal, 180th Quartermaster Battalion, MC.

Private 34624260 John Baswell, Jr. C Company, 4th Engineers Combat Battalion.

Private 1st Class 31132473 Warren D Cline, C Company, 4th Engineers Combat Battalion.

Private 31036404 Edmond Melanson, C Company, 4th Engineers Combat Battalion.

Private 38116593 Perry W Layfield, C Company, 4th Engineers Combat Battalion.

Technician 5th Class 14042533 Henry L Meggs, C Company, 4th Engineers Combat Battalion.

Private 7041483 Clyde Hardin, C Company, 4th Engineers Combat Battalion.

2nd Lieutenant O-528077 Charles A Carruth, C Company, 4th Engineers Combat Battalion.

Private 6992555 Clayton E Baker, C Company, 4th Engineers Combat Battalion.

Private 38404903 Glen J Whisenant, C Company, 4th Engineers Combat Battalion.

Lieutenant Colonel O-21839 Henry C Walker, lll, HQ 44th Field Artillery Battalion.

1st Lieutenant O-376854 Lambert C Root, HQ 44th Field Artillery Battalion.

Temporary Sergeant 20257778 James J O'Connor, Headquarters Battery, 480th AAA Automatic Weapons Battalion.

Private 1st Class 34093410 Daniel C Smith, Service Company, 29th Field Artillery Battalion.

Technician 5th Class 38319648 George E Hughes, A Company, 66th Armoured Regiment.

2 March 1944

Private 1st Class 13104513 Oliver C Saville, 1120th Military Police Company.

Technician 5th Class 31002560 John F MacPherson,

3473rd Ordnance Medium Automatic Maintenance Company.

Private 11000164 Wilfred D Lloyd, B Battery, 32nd Field Artillery Battalion.

Technician 4th Class 36162883 Robert J Earnshaw, 162nd Signals Photographic Company.

Private 34618119 Eugene Haynes, 433rd Engineer Tank Company.

4 March 1944

Staff Sergeant 33033935 Frank L Bowers, Headquarters 28th Infantry Regiment.

Private 1st Class 18003007 Oscar W Prudot, SOS (Infantry) Headquarter Company, Headquarters Command.

Technician 5th Class 17049733 Bernard Douvier, 131st Quartermaster Battalion.

Private 38267481 Wilson L Guidry, A Company, 146th Engineer Combat Battalion.

7 March 1944

Private 1st Class 14160608 Earl E Brooks, 1290th Military Police Company.

Private 13048652 Harry S Scott, 502nd Parachute Infantry Regiment, 1st Battalion.

Private 1st Class 14129952 Lawrence H Ward, 502nd Parachute Infantry Regiment, 1st Battalion.

Private 33559579 Henry J Lowry, Headquarters Company, 743rd Tank Battalion.

Private 33355738 Patrick J Boland, Headquarters Battery, 7th AAA Group.

Private 36188810 Rexford A Fingeroos, Headquarters Company, 2nd Battalion, 506th Parachute Infantry.

Technician 5th Class 32006010 Arthur T Goranson, 121st Signals Radio Int. Company.

Private 1st Class 6581704 Robert L Gilmour, 195th AAA Automatic Weapons Battalion.

Midshipman 3rd Class 608-97-45 Raymond E Becker, 2nd Beach Battalion, US Naval Reserve.

Private 31046495 Lee A Bosquet, C Company, 4th Engineers.

Technician 5th Class 32042911 Wesley R Gonyea, F Company, 8th Infantry.

Private 1st Class 35402431 Clyde B Elkins, C Company, 531st Engineer Regiment.

1st Sergeant 6806955 Thomas Evison, 42nd Field Artillery Battalion.

Private 1st Class 37294214 William L Waldock, F Company, 8th Infantry.

Private 33596053 Martin S Phillips, 875th Ordnance Company.

Master Sergeant 19076806 Ernest O Rockway, 1204th Quartermaster Service Group (was buried at Cambridge American Cemetery).

9 March 1944

Private 38277887 Horace L Gray, Service Battery, 183rd Field Artillery Battalion.

Private 1st Class John A Havelka, F Company, 36th Armoured Infantry Regiment, 3rd Armoured Division.

Private 337110651 Martin H O'Kada, F Company, 36th Armoured Infantry Regiment, 3rd Armoured Division.

11 March 1944

Technician 4th Class 31206044 Jasper M Blount, C Battery, 449th AAA, Automatic Weapons Battalion (was buried at Cambridge American Cemetery).

Private 1st Class 36043470 Henry Reasor, Service Company, 3rd Armoured Division.

Private 14035445 Earl V Sims, Service Company, 3rd Armoured Division.

14 March 1944

Private 35518086 John H Ruff, 803rd Chemical Company.

Mr Arnold E Bruhn, Pass Number 0-257912, a Civilian Technician, who was employed by the British & American Ordnance Company.

Private 1st Class 36578945 Francis R Almeida, A Battery, 430th AAA Battalion.

Private 32218018 Peter Psihogeos, C Company, 820th Engineer Battalion.

Private 36189358 Toivo M Stone, F Company, 39th Infantry Regiment, 9th Division.

Technician 4th Class Alexander M Shriver, Headquarters Battery, 224th Field Artillery Battalion.

Private 34142022 Charles C Bradley, 115th Infantry Regiment.

Company Warrant Officer W-2104557 Keith M Wakerman, Service Battery, 957th Field Artillery Battalion.

Staff Sergeant 20320703 Charles G Yeagley, Medium Det. 967th Field Artillery Battalion.

Private 1st Class 32162548 Isaac Lippert, Service Battery 967th Field Artillery Battalion.

Corporal 33036276 Alfred Vetturini, C Battery, 967th Field Artillery Battalion.

Private 32638227 Sidney C McClane, Service Battery, 967th Field Artillery Battalion.

Technician 5th Class 33035971 Ernest L Johnson, C Battery, 967th Field Artillery Battalion.

Technician 5th Class 32643010 Alexander Spitalnick, Med. Det. 967th Field Artillery Battalion.

16 March 1944

Private 33137886 Morris E McGirk, L Company, 3rd Battalion, 16th Infantry, 1st Division.

Private 35456693 Thomas W Partin, 1136th Quartermaster Company, 42nd Service Group.

Private 1st Class 38450796 Lloyd E Davis, B Company, 932nd Signals Battalion.

Private 34071131 Waymond Woods, 3264th Quartermaster Service Company.

Private 12188896 Melvin G Boaz, 43rd AD, Group.

Technician 5th Class 33158590 James R Thompson, B Company, 1340th Engineer Battalion, 1171st Group.

2nd Lieutenant O-1104450 John C Williams, B Company, 1340th Engineers Battalion, 1171st Group.

Sergeant 36364958 John O'Boyle, 2006th Ordnance Company (was buried at the Cambridge American Cemetery).

18 March 1944

Private 34610137 Joseph Benson, D Company, 366th Engineer General Service Regiment.

Seaman 2nd Class 313-04-52 Richard Hitchings, US Naval Reserve, USS-LST-*279* (LST-*279* arrived in England at Plymouth on 7 February 1944 and was engaged in numerous exercises in relation to amphibious landings around Plymouth, Salcombe and Dartmouth. In May 1944 she was assigned to the 28th Flotilla and placed under British operational control. On the morning of 7 June, LST-279 landed on the Green sector of Juno beach and dropped off British soldiers and their equipment before loading up with wounded soldiers and conveying them back to Portsmouth. Over the next couple of months she would make the return trip many times).

Boatswain 1st Class 341-93-55 Robert A Brown, US Navy.

Technician 5th Class 31093411 Frank W Hewlett, I Company, 531st Engineer Shore Regiment.

19 March 1944

Corporal 38444640 Elmer M Bryant, C Company, 850th Engineer Battalion (was buried at the Cambridge American Cemetery).

21 March 1944

Technician 5th Class 32241231 John Petruska, C Company, 707th Tank Battalion (was buried at the Cambridge American Cemetery).

Technician 4th Class 35649856 Charles E Hamlin, 3015th Quartermaster Bakery Company.

Private 35692623 Granville French, 4085th Quartermaster Service Company.

Private 1st Class 14028724 Rubin Harrison, Cannon Company, 47th Infantry.

Staff Sergeant 32014623 Moe Weiler, 9th Signal Company, 9th Infantry Division.

24 March 1944

Private 1st Class 35649576 John D Mitchell, A Company, 537th Quartermaster Battalion.

Technician 5th Class 31117468 Thomas J Albert, Service Battery 78th Armoured Field Artillery Battalion.

Technician 5th Class 38103049 Juan R Sapien, 65th Armoured Field Artillery Battalion.

Technician 4th Class 11096517 Oscar S Wischnowsky, 3262nd Ordnance Base Depot Company, 612th Ordnance, BAM.

25 March 1944

Technician 5th Class 33741102 Melvin R Chase, C Company 1314th Engineer Regiment.

26 March 1944

Private 16017167 Delbert G Hays, C Battery, 184th AAA, Gunnery Battalion.

Private 38052429 John L Mutina, I' Company, 16th Infantry.

Private 32825112 Anthony R Vergona, 346th Quartermaster Depot Company.

Private 20956524 William V Porter, Recon. Company, 803rd Tank Destroyer Battalion.

28 March 1944

Private 1st Class 20365665 William D Faidley, 29th Military Police Platoon, Special Troops, 29th Division.

Corporal 32637606 Frank J Monteforte, C Battery, 228th Field Artillery Battalion, XlX Corps.

Technician 5th Class 36524684 Raymond C Poirier, 773rd Tank Destroyer Battalion.

Sergeant 20342520 Charles F Stimax, H Company,115th Infantry, 29th Division.

The following eight men served with 1121st Quartermaster Company and were buried at the Cambridge American Cemetery. They were killed in a plane crash on 24 March 1944 when their B17 bomber crashed on takeoff near the village of Yeldom. The aircraft was heavily laden with bombs and a full tank of fuel; those on board didn't stand a chance. The crew of eleven also perished, along with two children on the ground.

Corporal 32450121 Sebastion J Attilio.

Private 32913998 Frank J Amato.

Technician 4th Class 31061256 Nils S Johnson.

Corporal 35355106 Robert P McClain.

Private 1st Class 13131672 Arnold N Chipoletti.

Private 1st Class 32498112 Michael R Arato.

Sergeant 37114308 Edward W Dell.

Private 33210046 William L Dickerson.

30 March 1944

2nd Lieutenant O-1824232 Anthony Romanelli, 771st Tank Destroyer Battalion.

Private 1st Class 31095321 Raymond C Ayotte, K Company, 116th Infantry.

Private 33017462 Vincent C Russell, Headquarters Company, 773rd Tank Destroyer Battalion.

Sergeant 34646420 Thomas E Garret, 3682nd Quartermaster Company.

Corporal 34483582 Lee E Johnson, 619th Ordnance Ammunition Company, 100th Battalion.

Private 1st Class 36001724 Charles S Skrabis, 1917th Ordnance Ammunition Company (was buried at the Cambridge American Cemetery).

Technician 5th Class 31330977 Raymond A Brundage, 1202nd Military Police Company (was also buried at the Cambridge American Cemetery).

1 April 1944

Private 1st Class 33068929 Frederick C Summers, 17th Armoured Engineer Battalion.

Private 1st Class 20613659 Charles W Griesman, 3815th Quartermaster Department.

4 April 1944

Technician 5th Class 34803293 Lewis M Morris, Headquarters 93rd Medium Gas Training Battalion.

Technician 4th Class 34042369 Joe West, 1st TD, GP.

Private 1214 1961 Private John Norwood, Medical Department, 48th General Hospital.

Private 36595786 James H Grenshaw, C Company, 234th Engineer Battalion.

Corporal 37507558 Edwin N Doering, 149th Engineer Combat Battalion.

Private 18163172 William L Banks, 467th Engineer

Maintenance Company.

Private 1206282 Raymond C Carlon, 531st Engineer (Shore Regiment).

6 April 1944

Technician 5th Class 13007652 Robert S Kistler, Headquarters Company, 9th Infantry Division.

Private 1st Class 37272320 John M Mintz, C Company, 743rd Tank Battalion, Infantry.

Private 35562074 Roy B Freed, C Company, 769th Military Police Battalion.

Private 1st Class 37264886 Alvin G Sunderman, 689th Ordnance Ammunition Company.

2nd Lieutenant 0-1016226 John W Vorhes, Jr. C Company, 743rd Tank Battalion, Infantry.

Private 38371552 Wilfred D Casson, C Battery, 552nd AAA Battalion.

Private 1st Class 35674214 Carl F Dahms, 33rd Signals Construction Battalion.

Private 39572511 George T Washington, 953rd Quartermaster Service Company.

Private 1st Class Eugene C Lamca, B Company, 203rd Engineer Combat Battalion.

1st Sergeant 32073341 Albert B Lewis, 24th Engineer Company.

Private 35597165 Elwood K Chain, 519th Ordnance Company.

Private 34557288 Jack Davis, 4149th Quartermaster Service Company.

8 April 1944

Private 34060356 Ben Bradley, D Company, 1314th Engineer Regiment.

Corporal 11014774 Charles H Wallace, 32nd Field Artillery Battalion, 1st Division.

Private 1st Class 33499714 Alfred J Sylvester, Headquarters Company, 397th AAA, Automatic Weapons Battalion.

11 April 1944

Technician 5th Class 31112101 Wilber S Munger, 91st M R U Infantry.

Private 35799631 William T Baldock, 959th Quartermaster Service Company.

Private 1st Class 15041955 Harvey B Sanders, H&S, 1278th Engineer Battalion.

Technician 5th Class 35169704 Marcus Bledstein, 286th Assault Signal Battalion, 1st Engineers Special Brigade.

1st Lieutenant Walter M Boland, H Company, 26th Infantry.

Having looked through all of the burial reports which were sent by the military authorities in England to the Quartermaster General in New York, I have found a total of 217 names of military personnel who died and were buried in England between January and May 1944. This list includes mainly army personnel who, because of the roles or work they were involved in, could have possibly been involved in the amphibious beach landing exercises which took place along the Devon coastline. This is an extremely high number of men for a nation to lose in training in such a short time, even for wartime.

It has to be said that during the time Exercise Duck (January 1944) and Exercise Fox (9 and 10 March) went ahead, there were no particularly large spikes of deaths. During the time of these two exercises there were allegedly friendly fire incidents which resulted in the deaths of hundreds of American servicemen.

The official records of deaths of American servicemen who were in England at the time certainly do not corroborate the claims that have been made about hundreds of Americans having been killed by friendly fire. This of course can mean only one of two things: either the alleged incidents did not happen, or that these incidents did take place and were covered up by the authorities. If the latter happened, this would mean that the bodies of these men must have been secretly buried somewhere, possibly in the Slapton Sands area, in unmarked mass graves, with their deaths then being explained away as casualties of the Normandy landings a couple of months later.

There has even been a suggestion that the bodies of a large number of American soldiers were brought to Portland and placed in the tunnels under the Verne, and that the bodies were still there as recently as 1994 when the tunnel entrances were blown up and sealed.

There have been many stories of American soldiers being buried in fields. One, on a website forum by the name of armchairgeneral.com, dated May 2014, tells the story of a man who was camping with a friend in 1969 when he was about 19 years old. While on holiday there they visited a pub that the man believed was called *The Sportsman's Arms*. He described it as being 'on a bend in the main road where a small lane came up from a village called Dittisham'. He got into a conversation with a group of elderly gents who started talking about a wartime exercise that had gone wrong and that a great many bodies had been quickly buried in a field directly behind the pub, and that they were still there, and that they were the only ones who knew about it.

There is a pub with the name *Sportsman's Arms* in Dittisham on the A3122.

While researching this book I came across many stories which had originated from ordinary people, men who had witnessed events all those years ago in the aftermath of Slapton Sands, Americans and British alike, men who didn't know each other, men who didn't have any reason to lie or make up stories, and men who knew what they had seen all those years ago and whose memories hadn't faded or been diminished over the course of time. What they had seen had stayed with them for the rest of their days, too horrible to ever be forgotten. If the events of 27 April 1944 never took place, then how come there are so many people who say that they did? They surely can't all be wrong, despite repeated denials by official bodies?

Sadly, with the passing of more than seventy years since the end of the Second World War, I do not believe that either the American or British authorities will ever now come out and admit what really happened at Slapton Sands or what happened to the bodies of the men who were killed there. To be clear, I am talking about the events of 27 April and not 28 April 1944.

Failure of the Normandy Landings, or if they had never taken place, would have meant a defeat from which the Allied nations might never have recovered. They have had no other option but to sue for peace with Nazi Germany, which would have brought an end to the war in Europe. I don't quite think it would have necessarily resulted in Britain having to surrender, because she still had the support of America and the other Commonwealth countries. But with Germany no longer having to worry about Britain and her Allies, she would have had large numbers of Allied prisoners under her control and also be in possession of large quantities of Allied vehicles, equipment.

It could have spelled trouble for Russia, with Germany then being in a position to concentrate more of her forces on the eastern front, resulting in a possible German victory.

It could also have meant long-term trouble for Japanese forces in the Pacific, as America, Britain and the Commonwealth forces would have more than likely focused all of their attention on them.

If Germany had defeated the Allies in Normandy but not gained a decisive victory, the atomic bombs that were dropped on Hiroshima and Nagasaki could have just as easily have been dropped on Berlin, Munich or Dresden. Then would Russian soldiers have stopped in Berlin, or would they have continued and taken over large swathes of Europe, with nothing to stop them?

Another scenario could have seen Germany and Japan joining forces and attacking America. With America defeated, an isolated Great Britain would not have been far behind.

A Nazi Germany in control of mainland Europe could have spelled the annihilation of the Jewish race throughout the continent, with possibly more to follow as the Nazis conquered more and more nations around the world.

Having considered those nightmare scenarios, one must conclude that the sacrifices made during that time, whether by the hundreds of young men who lost their lives during the training exercises, or the hundreds of people and families who left their homes so that American soldiers could train there, was worth it. If these sacrifices hadn't been made, and lessons hadn't been learnt, then the world might have had a totally different look to it today.

Sources

www.findagrave.com
Wikipedia
www.cwgc.com
www.britishnewspaperarchive.co.uk
www.historystockexchange.com
www.dday.com
www.hut-six.com
www.history.army.mil.co.uk
www.exercisetiger.org.uk
www.militaryfactory.com
www.ww2today.com

Index

✗PEN & SWORD BOOKS
ALSO AVAILABLE FROM
STEPHEN WYNN

BILLERICAY
IN THE
GREAT WAR

£12.99
9781783463404

LAINDON
IN THE
GREAT WAR

£12.99
9781783463657

BRENTWOOD
IN THE
GREAT WAR

£12.99
9781473822191

ROMFORD
IN THE
GREAT WAR

£12.99
9781473822207

GRAYS
(THURROCK)
IN THE
GREAT WAR

£12.99
9781473823105

CASTLE POINT
IN THE
GREAT WAR

£12.99
9781473823112

THE ISLE OF SHEPPEY
IN THE
GREAT WAR

£12.99
9781473834064

MAIDSTONE
IN THE
GREAT WAR

£12.99
9781473827912

CHATHAM
IN THE
GREAT WAR

£12.99
9781473827882

GRAVESEND
IN THE
GREAT WAR

£12.99
9781473827899

DARTFORD
IN THE
GREAT WAR

£12.99
9781473827905

FOLKESTONE
IN THE
GREAT WAR

£12.99
9781473827929

DOVER
IN THE
GREAT WAR

£12.99
9781473827936

DURHAM CITY
IN THE
GREAT WAR

£12.99
9781783030323

CITY OF
LONDON
IN THE
GREAT WAR

£12.99
9781473828599

TUNBRIDGE
WELLS
IN THE
GREAT WAR

£12.99
9781473833647

ISLE OF THANET
IN THE
GREAT WAR

£14.99
9781473834057

THE SURRENDER OF
SINGAPORE
THREE YEARS OF HELL

£19.99
9781473824027

WOMEN
in the
GREAT
WAR

£12.99
9781473834149

Against
All Odds
WALTER TULL

£16.99
9781526704047

FOR MORE INFORMATION VISIT: WWW.PEN-AND-SWORD.CO.UK
OR TO ORDER COPIES PLEASE CALL: 01226 734222